ORCHID
BASICS

Publishing Director: Alison Goff
Creative Director: Keith Martin
Executive Editor: Julian Brown
Editor: Karen O'Grady
Executive Art Editor: Mark Winwood
Design: Rozelle Bentheim
Picture Research: Sally Claxton
Production Controller: Lucy Woodhead
Cover Photography: Mark Winwood
Illustrator: Martin Jarman

First published in Great Britain in 2000
by Hamlyn,
This edition published 2004 by Bounty Books,
a division of Octopus Publishing Group Ltd,
2-4 Heron Quays, London E14 4JP

Copyright © 2000 Octopus Publishing Group Limited

ISBN 0 7537 0928 7

A catalogue record for this book is available from the British Library

Produced by Toppan
Printed in China

ORCHID
BASICS

Isobyl la Croix

Contents

Introduction

Many plants have their devotees, but few give rise to such passion as orchids. Why is it that people become obsessed? Their beauty, strangeness and mystique must all play a part but perhaps most of all, their sheer variety appeals. If you like large, brightly coloured flowers, what is more flamboyant than a *Cattleya* hybrid? If you prefer purity of form and colour, nothing can surpass *Angraecum* and *Aerangis*. On the other hand, if your taste runs to the bizarre, you are spoilt for choice; they come in all sizes from the huge flowers of *Stanhopea* to the small flowers of many *Bulbophyllum* species. Orchids also provide scented flowers; many are strongly scented, both during the day and in the evening. Furthermore, orchid growing is an all-year-round hobby – there is always something in flower.

People come to love orchids in many ways. Sometimes they visit a flower show and are captivated by an orchid display; in other cases they may receive one as a gift. But probably the most common way is by buying a plant in flower from a garden centre. If that does well, they may buy another and when the plants stop flowering, they will need to know how to bring them into flower again. This will lead them to buy a book or join an orchid society, and by that time, the orchid owner is hooked.

Most people start with a general collection, acquiring any plants they can. But often, possibly for reasons of space, they start to specialize in a particular kind of orchid that grows well in the conditions they have on offer, perhaps African orchids, scented orchids, miniature orchids or a genus such as *Phalaenopsis*. Many growers have a well-developed collector's instinct, and try to amass as many of a particular genus or group as possible, but others just enjoy the beauty of their plants – and usually in a warm, pleasant environment rather than a wet and windswept garden.

Orchids have been cultivated in China for as long as 3,000 years but, as far as we know, the first tropical orchid to be grown in Europe was the South and Central American species *Brassavola nodosa*, in the late 17th century. In Britain, orchids first appeared in cultivation in the 18th century. William Aiton, Superintendent of the famous Kew Gardens, produced *Hortus Kewensis*, a three-volume catalogue of plants growing in Kew Gardens. This was first published in 1789 and lists 15 species of exotic orchid, while the second edition, published in 1813, includes no less than 70 species.

Initially, growers had little success in keeping these orchids alive. Because they were tropical plants they were grown in stove houses, where the atmosphere was hot but dry. No one knew that many came from high altitudes and required cool, moist conditions. Gradually, however, often by trial and error, gardeners came to realize that not all tropical orchids needed high temperatures, but almost all did need a good level of humidity and plenty of ventilation, and before long some large collections were built up. It must be remembered, too, that before the days of air travel, orchids had to undertake long sea voyages to reach European shores and many would already be in poor condition by the time they reached the boat.

Nowadays, collecting orchids in the wild is, or is supposed to be, strictly controlled and almost all cultivated orchids are grown from seed or produced by meristem culture. Apart from preserving wild stock, these plants are in fact much better suited to greenhouse or windowsill cultivation.

Now that their needs are understood, it is a myth that orchids are difficult to grow. A few may be, but most are not and in fact they can be surprisingly difficult to kill. No one can hope to grow all varieties of orchids equally well, but by observing a few simple rules the majority are no more difficult than any other houseplant. It is another myth that they are expensive. Again, some are and wildly inflated prices for a particularly rare or desirable variety help to perpetuate this myth. However, mass production has brought the prices of popular varieties within reach of everyone, making orchids an affordable and immensely enjoyable hobby for all.

Brassavola nodosa was the first tropical orchid to be grown in Britain.

The orchid family, Orchidaceae, is probably the largest family of flowering plants in the world; with over 20,000 species in over 700 genera, its only possible rival is the daisy family, Compositae. Many orchid genera contain only one species but others are very large, for example *Bulbophyllum*, *Dendrobium*, *Epidendrum* and *Pleurothallis* are each thought to contain over 1,000 species. This may seem strange as orchids are often considered to be rare plants, and indeed many are confined to limited areas and specific habitats and consequently are at great risk from destruction of these habitats. Even common orchids tend to be local in their occurrence and do not dominate the vegetation in the way that certain other plants do.

The orchid family

1

The orchid family

What is an orchid?

Why is an orchid an orchid – what are the distinctive features? Orchids are related to plants such as lilies. Like lilies, orchid flowers have three sepals and three petals but one of the petals, known as the lip or labellum, is always modified in some way. Often it is larger than the other petals and of a different shape or colour, sometimes marked with lines and blotches. In some orchids, for example *Cyrtorchis*, the lip is similar in appearance to the other petals but it carries a nectar-bearing spur at the base. Another distinctive feature is the reproductive parts of an orchid flower. The stamens, style and stigma (see page 46) are joined together to form a structure called the column, usually easily seen in the centre of the flower. In other plants, these structures are separate. Also, orchid pollen, instead of being loose as in most other plants, is joined into masses called pollinia.

Where orchids grow

Orchids can be found on every continent except Antarctica; some even grow inside the Arctic Circle. Between half and three-quarters of orchids are epiphytic, which means that they grow on other plants; the rest, including all native European species, are terrestrial, which means they grow on the ground. Epiphytes do not take any nutrients from their host – they simply use the host plant as a support or platform. It seems probable that orchids took to the trees to be nearer the light; the floor of a tropical forest is very dark and while some species became adapted to cope with these conditions, others moved upwards. It is easy to see how the habit

Epiphytic orchids in the wild.

developed: in the tropics, certain species that usually grow in leaf litter on the forest floor may sometimes be seen growing low down on tree trunks or in the forks of trees.

Orchids, of course, are not the only kind of epiphytic plant – in South American forests, bromeliads (often grown as air plants) are an important part of the epiphytic flora, and epiphytic ferns can be found all over the world. Some orchids grow on rocks and are known as lithophytes, but few species are consistently lithophytic. In the wild it is not uncommon to see a certain type of orchid growing on a tree, and nearby the same species flourishing on a rock. Terrestrial orchids may also grow on rocks on occasions, although in this case the roots or tubers are usually embedded in a layer of moss or humus rather than directly attached to the rock.

Epiphytic orchids

Most orchid species and the hybrids derived from them are tropical epiphytes. These plants have become adapted to their lifestyle in several ways, notably in their roots. Many have thick roots that fulfil a double function; as well as anchoring the plant to the branch or rock, the roots are surrounded by layers of dead cells called the velamen, which

Polystachya brassii growing on a rock; it can also grow on trees.

readily absorb any available moisture. Even in tropical rainforests there is usually a dry season and in many places where orchids grow, the dry season can be quite severe. So epiphytic orchids are adapted in various ways to enable them to survive a period of drought, including their thick, leathery leaves that prevent moisture loss and their swollen stem bases, known as pseudobulbs, which also help conserve moisture.

How epiphytic orchids grow

Epiphytic orchids have two basic growth patterns: they may be monopodial or sympodial.

Monopodial These orchids have a leafy stem that grows continuously from the top although it may branch, usually at the base. This does not necessarily mean that these are tall plants; in many the amount of annual growth is very small and they remain compact. The flowers develop along the stems, usually in the leaf axils, and roots can also arise along the stem as well as at the base of the plant. After the resting season, growth resumes at the top of the stem. Monopodial orchids include vandas, phalaenopsis and angraecums.

Angraecum birrimense is a monopodial or vandoid orchid.

Sympodial Sympodial orchids have a creeping rhizome (a horizontal stem growing either on or below the ground) with one or more new shoots arising

A new shoot grows from last year's pseudobulbs.

Slender pseudobulbs of *Dendrochilum javierense*.

from it each year. The flower spike often grows from the end of the stem, although it may arise at the base of the plant, beside the leafy growth. Most, but not all, sympodial orchids have pseudo-bulbs (swollen stem bases) which vary greatly in shape, size and arrangement. They may be large or small, round, ovoid, spindle-shaped or cane-like and may be set well apart on the creeping rhizome,

Ridged, conical pseudobulbs set close together.

form clumps or grow from the previous year's pseudobulb and form a chain. Whatever the shape, pseudobulbs remain on the plant for several years, even after the leaves have been shed, and seem to have a storage function.

Terrestrial orchids

Terrestrial orchids also have different growth patterns. Some have creeping stems on or just below ground level with roots and clusters of leaves growing from them which may last for one or more years. The jewel orchids have this type of growth. Most terrestrial orchids have some sort of underground storage organ that keeps the plant alive while it is dormant. The dormant, or resting, season is winter in cool temperate climates, the hot dry summer in parts of the world with a Mediterranean-type climate, or the dry season in the tropics. The storage organs may be fleshy roots,,

Dactylorhiza foliosa, the Madeira orchid, adds rich colour to a garden.

The Common Spotted Orchid, *Dactylorhiza fuchsii*, is widespread in Europe.

corms, tubers or pseudobulbs that are often partly above ground. Corms and pseudobulbs persist for several years, sometimes forming long chains, but tubers and fleshy roots are usually renewed each year.

Orchids in the wild

While it is never possible to reproduce exactly the conditions in which orchids grow in the wild, it helps to know what these conditions are. For example, as we have seen, in the early days of orchid growing most imported species died because they were grown in a hot, dry atmosphere. Once it was known that many orchids, although they came from the tropics, are high-altitude plants used to relatively cool, moist conditions, things began to improve.

Epiphytic orchids in the wild
Epiphytic orchids are naturally forest or woodland plants. This is why so many orchids are endangered, as all over the world, tropical forest and woodland is being felled for fuel or to clear land for farming. It follows that most are shade-loving plants – few like full exposure to sunlight. Some grow in surprisingly dark conditions, such as low down on tree trunks in dense forest, and even those that grow high up in the branches get some shade from the leafy canopy. In the wild, few orchids grow where the dry season is long and severe but almost all have to survive some period of relatively adverse conditions. So in cultivation almost all benefit from a rest when they are kept cooler and drier than when in active growth, and in fact many will not flower without such a rest. As a general rule, the thicker an orchid's roots, the less water it needs when not in active growth. Most orchids with fine roots, particularly those without pseudobulbs, are forest plants used to a short dry season.

Terrestrial orchids in the wild
Terrestrial orchids occur in a great range of habitats. The only common factor is that few, if any, can cope with competition from other plants. If grass is not kept short by grazing or controlled cutting, scrub develops and the orchids vanish.

In equatorial regions there are more epiphytic orchids than terrestrial but the further one moves from the equator, the higher the proportion of terrestrials. Few terrestrial orchids grow in the deep shade of the tropical forest floor but some do and this gives a clue to the conditions they like – warm, humid and shady. More can be found in open woodland, usually where the soil is poor and stony, but probably most species occur in grassland. Such plants do not take well to cultivation so they should only be attempted by the skilled grower, and in any case, most are difficult to obtain.

Orchid conservation

Many species of orchid have suffered greatly from over-collecting and some are even believed to be extinct in the wild. In an attempt to combat this, all orchids, both species and hybrids, are covered by the Convention on International Trade in Endangered Species (CITES). This means that orchid plants may not be brought or sent from one country to another without an import permit issued by the importing country and an export permit from the country of export. Free movement is, however, allowed within countries belonging to the European Union. A health certificate is also required. Furthermore, almost all countries have their own laws forbidding collection of wild orchids. Orchid seedlings in flasks (see page 48), however, are exempt from CITES regulations and do not need a health certificate.

Orchid names

Only a few orchids have a common name and even when they do, it tends to be a name for a group rather than for a particular species.
For example,
Miltoniopsis hybrids
are known as pansy orchids,
Phalaenopsis
are known as moth orchids and
Coryanthes
are known as bucket orchids.

So even a beginner has to become familiar with the botanical names.

Plant names are covered by a Code of Nomenclature. Orchid species, like other plants, have two names.

The first name, **the generic name**, begins with a capital letter and is given to all plants in the same genus, for example *Angraecum*.
The second name is **the specific name** and belongs to one species, for example *eburneum*, which is the specific name of the orchid *Angraecum eburneum*.
There may be, in addition, subspecies or varieties –
we can have
Angraecum eburneum subsp. *eburneum*;
Angraecum eburneum subsp. *giryamae*
and
Angraecum eburneum subsp. *superbum*.
There is even
Angraecum eburneum subsp. *superbum* var. *longicalcar*.

The naming of hybrids is explained in Chapter 6.

Awards

Plants offered for sale may have letters after the name, such as FCC, AM or HCC. The first stands for First Class Certificate and is the highest award; AM is Award of Merit and is the next highest; HCC stands for Highly Commended Certificate. These awards are given by judging authorities such as the Royal Horticultural Society (RHS) and the American Orchid Society (AOS) – in these cases, the initials RHS or AOS should come after the award. Awards are an indication of quality and are given to a particular plant and not to the species or hybrid as a whole and so any awarded plant must have a cultivar name which begins with a capital letter and is enclosed in single quotation marks; for example, *Epidendrum revolutum* 'Burnham' AM/RHS and *Pleione* Shantung 'Ridgeway' AM/RHS..

Orchids can be grown in many places: in a greenhouse, on a windowsill, in a special case or under artificial lights, say, in a basement. In the tropics they can be grown in a shade house or in the garden. Orchids, like other plants, need water, light, nutrients and an adequate temperature if they are to thrive. If the grower can provide the right requirements, no matter where, the plants should be successful.

Where to grow orchids

2

Where to grow orchids

Greenhouses

A greenhouse is probably the most popular place to grow orchids. Sometimes there will be an existing greenhouse in the garden, but often the new grower has to build one and in that case there are choices to be made. Greenhouses can have metal or wooden frames, have glass to the ground or solid walls at the base, and be glazed with glass or polycarbonate. Each type has its advantages and disadvantages. Wooden structures tend to look more attractive and it is easier to fix things like insulation and electrical appliances to the walls but they are more expensive to buy, require more maintenance and are more difficult to clean. Solid walls up to staging level are more heat-efficient but the lack of light low down means that plants cannot be grown under the staging.

A prospective purchaser should look at catalogues from a number of greenhouse suppliers, but the most important thing is to visit orchid houses and talk to growers to determine what is likely to suit best. Whatever type of greenhouse you choose, it is a good idea to buy the biggest you can afford and accommodate. The smaller the greenhouse, the greater is the surface area to volume ratio and the more difficult it is to maintain a stable temperature. Do not think that as you have only a few plants, you only need a small greenhouse – filling the space will be the least of your problems. Consider a minimum of 3 x 2.4m (10 x 8ft), and if possible have one that is 3.6m (12ft) wide, so that another block of staging can be fitted in the centre to give a more efficient use of space.

Orchids growing in a metal framed greenhouse

Cymbidiums in a greenhouse.

Siting a greenhouse

Siting a greenhouse is usually a matter for compromise. Ideally, it should not be overhung by large trees, the long axis should run east to west and it should be close enough to the house to have its own electrical and water supplies. But such a site is rarely found in a garden. Sometimes a lean-to greenhouse is the only option.

Greenhouse manufacturers advise that the corner posts should be set in concrete, but it is a good idea to have the whole greenhouse anchored in a concrete base. Apart from the extra strength – essential in exposed areas – a concrete base makes it more difficult for slugs, snails, mice and other such unwelcome visitors to enter.

Glazing materials and insulation

Glass is still the most widely used glazing material but polycarbonate sheeting has many advantages: it is lighter, virtually unbreakable and can be used as a double layer to give built-in insulation. However, it is still more expensive than glass. Other clear plastic materials are not suitable as they become cloudy and denatured after a few years. It is possible to have glass double glazing but this is very heavy and would probably require a specially designed building. Otherwise, glass greenhouses need some form of insulation to keep heating costs down. The most widely used is bubble poly-thene, which is attached to the inside of the greenhouse. It can be tacked to the frame of a wooden greenhouse; metal greenhouses have grooves in the frame and special plastic pegs are used to fix the lining. Bubble polythene is available in rolls in a choice of widths, together with the pegs and strong adhesive tape. It is available with large or small bubbles; the former is more effective. Unfortun-ately polythene has a limited life, up to about seven years; it then starts to break up and has to be replaced.

Heating methods

After deciding on the type of greenhouse to buy, the next step is to decide how to heat it. Again, each method has advan-tages and drawbacks. Electricity is the most widely used; it is usually the cheapest to install, is the cleanest and most convenient and offers the most control. The drawbacks are that it can be expensive to run, particularly in a large greenhouse, and of all the methods, it is the most likely to fail. The days of power cuts may be past but winter storms still take their toll.

In the early days of orchid growing, greenhouses had hot-water pipes run-ning under the staging, heated by a solid-fuel boiler. Hot water pipes still offer a good form of heating, providing an even heat that does not give off fumes or dry out the air too much. These pipes come in two diameters, 10cm (4in) and 5cm (2in). The narrower pipes give a faster response but need an electric pump to circulate the water. Water in the larger pipes circulates by convection, and the pipes retain heat longer.

Oil-fired and gas-fired greenhouse boilers are available and although the initial cost may be higher, running costs should be lower than with electricity. As long as the boiler is gravity fed and does not require an electric pump, it will keep going even if the electric power supply fails and as hot-water pipes retain their heat for several hours, there is no sud-den loss of temperature if something goes wrong. These boilers have controls but they are not as flexible as the control available with electrical heating.

If a greenhouse is very near or attached to a house, it is a good idea to heat it through the house central heating as long as the system is not set to switch off at night.

Back-up heating

Whatever method is used, it is almost certain to fail at some time and it is essential to have some other kind of heating in reserve, as a whole collection of orchids can be lost overnight. With gas- or oil-fired systems, electric fan-heaters can serve as a back-up. Otherwise, paraffin or bottled gas heaters can be kept for use in an emergency.

Shading

Few orchids enjoy strong light so some sort of shading is necessary in the summer months and this also helps to prevent overheating. The cheapest and easiest method of shading is to paint the glass white; special paints for this are available from most garden centres. These paints are water resistant, but are easily rubbed off. Shade cloth or lath blinds are also effective and are most efficient when fixed to the outside of the house and raised above the glass, but this is not too easy to arrange and is not practical in a windy area.

Ventilation

In the wild, epiphytic orchids grow in airy places and good air movement in a greenhouse leads to better growth and fewer problems with fungus. All greenhouses have vents in the roof and these can be automatically controlled so that the plants can be left for a day or more without the worry of overheating, or of sudden draughts should the weather change for the worse. Automatic vents are usually available from the greenhouse manufacturer as an optional extra. They do not need a supply of electricity; simple and effective kinds operate using bimetallic strips or oil-filled cylinders.

One or two fans are also beneficial in a greenhouse, ideally sited over a pathway so that the moving air does not blow directly on to the plants. Fan heaters are a good investment as they can be set to heat the greenhouse or merely to move the air about to provide ventilation without additional heat.

Humidity

Almost all orchids like high humidity and this can be difficult to achieve especially in summer when the air is warm and the greenhouse vents are open. The old-fashioned method of raising humidity is by 'damping down'; the floor and under staging is sprayed with water and as this evaporates, the humidity rises. This method can still be used today if a greenhouse has no electrical supply.

However, various kinds of automatic humidifiers are available. Ultrasonic nebulizers were originally designed to create a humid atmosphere for asthma sufferers and give off a cloud of what looks like cold steam, but they do not cover a very large area and so are better suited to small greenhouses. The drawbacks are that they are fairly bulky, and if they are working consistently, the water reservoir can run out in less than a day. Also the filters need to be cleaned regularly as they get clogged up. Other systems available run from the mains water supply and consist of a series of mist jets. Fine jets can be positioned wherever they are required and it is possible to control the level of relative humidity at which they come on. The advantage of these systems is that they keep going if the owner is away. The finer the jet the better, and they should not play directly on to plants in pots as soggy compost soon leads to rot. Mounted plants love it, however.

Lighting

Extra lighting is also an option in a greenhouse. It is useful for extending the day length and thus encouraging growth in winter, particularly when the winter day is very short. Ordinary white fluorescent tubes can be used. This subject is dealt with on page 22.

Alpine houses

Alpine houses differ from standard greenhouses in having extra vents near the base of the house; they are either completely unheated or just kept free of frost in winter. Quite a lot of orchids can be grown in a frost-free alpine house, including pleiones and Mediterranean species such as *Ophrys*. With many near-hardy orchids, it is not the cold but the wet that kills them in the open garden, so a cool alpine house can provide the perfect conditions. For more details, see Chapter 10.

Bletilla striata can be grown in the garden or in an alpine house.

Staging

All greenhouses and alpine houses need staging and again there is a range of types available. Staging should not be too wide or it is difficult to reach plants at the back although tiered staging makes this easier. Slatted staging gives the free drainage that orchids like but the slats should not be set too far apart as a lot of orchids are grown in small pots.

Windowsills

Most people grow their first orchid with other houseplants on a windowsill and, if it is successful, they will acquire more orchids. At this stage, many people decide to invest in a greenhouse but others continue to grow large collections in the house, often very successfully. Temperature is seldom a problem here; the most difficult aspect is providing sufficient humidity without the walls and curtains sprouting green mould.

Kitchens and bathrooms are favoured places for indoor orchids as they tend to have higher humidity than other rooms, but orchids can be grown in any room that is warm enough. The usual solution is to have the pots sitting on trays containing a layer of moisture-retentive material, such as expanded clay pellets or perlag. This gives a humid atmosphere round the plants but the pots sit on the pellets, not in the water, thus preventing the soil from becoming waterlogged. It is always better to arrange orchids in groups rather than singly, as plants create their own humidity.

In the Northern Hemisphere, site plants close to an east- or west-facing window as a south-facing window is likely to be too hot in summer although

Cymbidium hybrids do well as house plants.

good in winter. Net curtains will help to screen the scorching effects of direct sun or plants can, of course, be placed on a table set back slightly from the window – a bay window is particularly suitable for this. It goes without saying that the window should not be draughty. Orchids should not be put on top of a radiator or a television set where they will get too hot and dry. For obvious reasons, miniature orchids are best suited for house culture. A list of suitable species is given below, although many others could well be successful.

Plants to grow on a windowsill

Aerangis fastuosa
Angraecum didieri and *rutenbergianum*
Brassavola nodosa
Cattleya intermedia and *skinneri*
Cattleya hybrids, particularly

'mini-cattleyas'
Coelogyne cristata and *nitida*
Cymbidium devonianum and
  floribundum
Cymbidium miniature hybrids
Dendrobium kingianum
Dendrobium nobile and hybrids
Encyclia cochleata and *vitellina*
Laelia anceps and *gouldiana*
Ludisia discolor
Masdevallia species and hybrids
Maxillaria tenuifolia
Paphiopedilum callosum
Phalaenopsis hybrids
Pleione species and hybrids
Stenoglottis species

Artificial lights

The practice of growing orchids under artificial lights seems to be more common in America than in Europe. It enables parts of a house such as a basement, cellar or loft to be used as a growing area. This has much to recommend it as the area is likely to be heated to some extent already and, being enclosed, it will tend to have a fairly high humidity. Growing orchids under lights gives the grower almost complete control over growing conditions. It is possible to have a day length of 12–16 hours all year round so that plants grow continuously, although this would be better for young stock than for mature flowering plants, where some seasonal variation is desirable.

It is possible to buy 'grow lights' specially formulated for optimum plant growth. However, the blue and red parts of the spectrum are the wavelengths mainly used in photosynthesis (the process by which green plants use light to produce energy) and these are supplied by white fluorescent tubes. Ordinary incandescent light bulbs give light in the red part of the spectrum, which helps to trigger flowering, and so a combination of the two kinds should give good results. Four 40-watt fluorescent tubes and four 8-watt incandescent bulbs would be a suitable arrangement. The lights are usually fixed on to a piece of wood that is suspended on chains from the ceiling, allowing them to be moved up and down. The lights should be 15–45cm (6–18in) above the leaves; obviously light-loving orchids such as *Cattleya* should be positioned near the lights and those that prefer more shade, such as *Phalaenopsis*, should be further away. Remember that lights also give off heat. In any enclosed area ventilation is essential, and fan heaters are most suitable for this.

Orchid cases

Orchid cases are direct descendants of the glass Wardian cases that were first used in the mid-19th century to improve survival rates of orchids and other plants which had to endure long sea voyages. In 1842, the English nursery firm Loddiges said that after they started using Wardian cases, the survival rate of imported plants rose from five per cent to ninety-five per cent.

As these cases obviously provided excellent growing conditions, they began to be used in other ways and in late Victorian times they became very fashionable. By this time, Wardian cases had changed from the original wooden glass-topped boxes to decorative structures, usually entirely of glass, often in elaborate shapes such as a miniature model of the Crystal Palace in South

Orchid cases can make an attractive feature in a room.

London. Not many of these survive and those that do are collectors' pieces, but simpler cases are still used to grow orchids successfully and make a decorative feature in a living room. Heat, light and humidity can be controlled automatically in such cases.

A small orchid collection can be grown entirely in this way, and people with larger collections sometimes use them for difficult species that need carefully controlled conditions, as well as for their decorative effect. Few, if any, firms still make orchid cases, but they are still occasionally available second-hand. Otherwise, it is not too difficult to have one made; a number of firms could supply the necessary controls. A typical size is about 1.5m (5ft) high by 1.2m (4ft) wide and 60cm (24in) deep – these are the outside measurements; the growing area is slightly smaller. The floor of such

cases usually consists of a waterproof tray with aggregate granules under which there is a heating cable set on a wooden base with a movable grill to control air flow. The wooden roof has vent holes but a small fan may also be necessary as good ventilation is essential. For a cabinet of this size, three 40-watt fluorescent tubes should be sufficient; they can be controlled by a time switch set to give 12–14 hours of light a day. Keep 2.5cm (1in) of water in the tray to keep the humidity high.

Plants to grow in an orchid case
Aerangis, most species
Angraecum, smaller species
Cattleya, small hybrids
Dendrobium bigibbum
Dendrobium hybrids
Dracula species
Ludisia discolor and other jewel orchids
Paphiopedilum, most species and
  hybrids
Phalaenopsis species and hybrids
Pleurothallis species

Shade houses

Shade houses are used for growing orchids in tropical and subtropical climates where the problem is one of too much heat and light, rather than cold. They are usually simple structures made from poles with a thatched or shade-cloth roof, often with shade-cloth or polythene curtains on the sides that catch the sun. They have the great advantage of being easy and cheap to extend when the need arises.

Given the right conditions, most orchids are no more difficult to grow than other plants. They can be grown in pots, in baskets or mounted on bark or tree fern slabs. Pots may be plastic or clay. Nowadays, plastic pots are more often used as they are cheaper, lighter and easier to clean and it is easier to get an orchid out when repotting as the roots do not cling so tightly to plastic as they do to clay. Terrestrial orchids, however, which are particularly sensitive to overwatering, do better in clay pots as the soil dries out much more quickly.

How to grow orchids

3

How to grow orchids

As growers become more involved in their hobby, they want to add all sorts of refinements, especially if they have a greenhouse. It is possible to grow orchids in a completely automated way, but this should not be at the expense of giving the plants personal attention. There is no substitute for the grower's eye. Automatic systems are useful, however, as they make it possible for the grower to go away without making complicated arrangements with neighbours to look after the plants.

Epiphytic orchids

Most epiphytic orchids can be grown in pots. It is often suggested that extra holes be drilled or burnt in pots to improve the drainage, but adding a layer of drainage material such as polystyrene chips in the bottom of the pot is just as effective. Baskets and rafts are useful where a plant has a creeping habit and keeps climbing out of a pot – cattleyas and many *Bulbophyllum* species behave like this.

Baskets

Baskets are essential for orchids such as stanhopeas where the flower spike actually grows downwards from the roots. Draculas have the same habit but as they are small plants with wiry flower spikes, a plastic mesh pot is often used. Baskets are also often used for orchids such as vandas with long, vigorous roots – in fact, vandas are sometimes grown in empty baskets with no compost at all. Wooden baskets can be bought but are very easy to make at home.

Mounts

Mounts are used for smaller plants that do not like to have their roots

Many orchids do well in a wooden basket.

confined in pots, such as most species of *Mystacidium*, and for plants with long-spurred flowers, such as *Aerangis* species.

Mounts and rafts can be made of a variety of materials such as slabs of cork, fir or pine bark, pieces of tree fern or small branches. Pieces of cork bark are the most traditional. They can often be bought from a florist, but are becoming expensive; thick pine bark that has separated from the outside of a log of firewood, can be equally good. The bark should be at least 1cm (½in) thick or it will not last. Bore a hole at one end and fit a neat wire hook through it so that the mount with its plant can be hung up in a shaded, humid place.

When pieces of wood are used as mounts, people tend to have their own favourites – some swear by apple, others by gorse. Most orchids prefer a textured piece where the roots can make their

Mounted orchids must be
firmly tied to the bark.

way into crevices, but a few species pre-fer smooth bark such as birch, or even a plain wood surface. Driftwood looks attractive, but if it comes from the sea, all the salt must be washed or weathered out. When an orchid outgrows its mount, the whole arrangement can be tied on to a larger mount.

When mounting a plant, fasten it on firmly – if the roots can move about, they are less likely to adhere to the bark. Various materials are used to tie orchids to their mounts. Fishing line is popular as it is very unobtrusive, but it can be diffi-cult to handle and there is always the possibility of it cutting into stems or roots as they grow thicker. String is a good alternative; it has a limited life but usually by the time it has rotted, the orchid has

become firmly attached and no longer needs it. Thin strips cut from tights or stockings are also good, but raffia rots too quickly. Mounted orchids need higher humidity than plants in pots because they have no compost from which to draw moisture, so it is helpful to place a small piece of moss behind the plant to keep it moist until it is established.

Potting composts

Bark mixes While orchids can be grown in all sorts of media, including coir, sphagnum moss and perlite, the most frequently used composts are based on chopped bark. Special orchid bark must be used. The partly composted bark that is sold as a mulch in garden centres is not suitable. Orchid bark is available in three grades. Fine grade is used for seedlings and often as part of other mixes; medium or standard grade is used for most flowering-size orchids and coarse grade is used for large, thick-rooted plants. It is advisable to wash or sieve the bark before using it to get rid of the powdery dust that always seems to be present to some extent. Bark can be used on its own but composts are usu-ally a mixture of bark, perlag or super-coarse perlite, and horticultural grade charcoal; they can be bought ready mixed or the grower can mix up his own.

Every 'recipe' seems to use these ingredients in slightly different propor-tions and it is not necessary to be too exact. A good mixture is six parts of bark to one part of coarse perlite and one part of charcoal. Sometimes coarse peat or chopped sphagnum moss is included, but this makes the mixture very water retentive, so care must be taken not to overwater.

For orchids past the seedling stage, mixes based on medium bark are most suitable, unless the roots are very fine. Whether coarse or fine, there should be free, open drainage and as soon as the compost shows signs of starting to de-compose, the plant should be repotted.

Almost all orchid houses become populated with ferns; under the staging, they are attractive and help to keep up humidity but do not let them grow in orchid pots as fern roots break down bark and the compost soon becomes a soggy mess. Moss is also undesirable in a pot (although acceptable, within rea-son, on a mount) as it tends to draw all the moisture from the compost.

Rockwool This is becoming increas-ingly popular as a potting mix. It is spun from molten volcanic rock, rather like fibreglass, and as it does not decompose like an organic mix, repotting should be necessary only when a plant outgrows its pot. Repotting from and into rockwool causes less disturbance than with bark-based mixes as the roots do not need to have all the old mixture shaken off.

Rockwool can be bought on its own in water-repellent and water-absorbent forms, but it is easier to buy it ready mixed as a complete potting mixture. Some mixtures also contain perlite. If perlite is not already included, add 30-50 per cent to the mixture to improve aera-tion. This will make the potting mix dry out quickly, so be vigilant with watering and do not have orchids growing in rockwool on the same bench as orchids growing in a bark mixture; the watering requirements are too different. If you wish to use both media, keep the plants in separate groups to avoid over- or underwatering. Rockwool supplies no nutrients at all so add fertilizer regularly.

Pterostylis curta is a popular species of terrestrial orchid.

Terrestrial orchids

Although less common in collections than epiphytes, some terrestrial orchids are widely cultivated, such as *Calanthe* and *Disa* hybrids which are becoming steadily more popular.

Growers who specialize in terrestrial orchids say that they are no more diffi-cult than epiphytes, but not everyone agrees. An epiphytic orchid is visible all year round and it is usually easy to see if there is something wrong, while most terrestrials disappear completely under-ground when they are dormant. When growing terrestrial orchids it is essential to follow the plant's natural rhythm. A few species are evergreen but most are deciduous and usually the leaves start to turn yellow and die back after flowering; this is a signal that the plant is ready to go into its resting period and should be kept dry.

Sprinkle some water on the surface every week or so during the dormant period or the tubers will shrivel, but don't start watering properly until the new shoots have grown 2.5cm (1in) above ground. Then carefully apply the water using a can with a fine spout – if any gets on to the new growth it is likely to turn black.

If you use clay pots to grow terrestrial orchids, plunge them in sand; during dormancy, keep the sand damp to provide enough moisture to stop roots or tubers from shrivelling, but not enough to make them rot.

Potting composts for terrestrial orchids

Various composts are recommended for terrestrial orchids but the exact ingredients are less important than the fact that they must be free draining – even species that grow in bogs and marshes in the wild will die if kept constantly wet in cultivation. Overwatering is the most common cause of death of terrestrial orchids; it is a useful rule to allow the compost to dry out before watering again. More or less the same ingredients occur in the suggested compost mixes, so obviously a fair bit of flexibility is possible. Disas, however, are a special case; their requirements are given later (see page 64).

Mix 1
1 part peat or peat substitute
1 part sterile loam
1 part coarse sand

Mix 2
2 parts sphagnum moss peat
1 part coarse sand
1 part perlite

Mix 3
3 parts sterile loam
3 parts coarse sand or grit
2 parts sieved beech or oak leaf mould
1 part fine orchid bark

Mix 4
3 parts fibrous peat
2 parts coarse perlite
2 parts coarse grit
1 part horticultural grade charcoal

Temperature

Orchids are classified by the temperatures that they require to grow successfully and are divided into warm, intermediate and cool. Warm-growing orchids require a night-time minimum temperature of 18°C (65°F) and, ideally, a daytime maximum of 27°C (80°F). Intermediate orchids need a night-time minimum of 13–15° (55–60°F) and an ideal maximum of 27°C (80°F). Cool-growing orchids require a minimum of about 10°C (50°F) with a maximum of 21°C (70°F). For any group, if the temperature occasionally falls a few degrees below the minimum it is unlikely to do harm, but it must be remembered that the cooler it is, the drier the plants should be kept. There should be a daytime rise in temperature of at least 5°C (10°F) although a short spell without this should not be harmful – it can be difficult to get much rise in a cold, dull spell in winter.

Maximum temperature is often more difficult to control than minimum and most orchids suffer in temperatures of over 35°C (95°F); it is best not to let it rise much over 30°C (86°F). At these high temperatures, high humidity is very important and frequent damping down and spraying also has a cooling effect.

With electrical heating systems, it is possible to control temperature very accurately, less so with systems which depend on hot-water pipes, which seem to have a particular range at which they run best. For example, in our greenhouse, a system using 10cm (4in) hot-water pipes heated by a gravity-fed, oil-fired boiler naturally gave intermediate conditions.

A large orchid house may be divided into cool, intermediate and warm sections, but this is rarely possible for the amateur grower, who must choose their temperature. The widest range of orchids can be grown in an intermediate house. All greenhouses, whatever their basic temperature, have warmer and cooler spots and the observant grower soon finds these out. By careful positioning and a bit of trial and error, you may be able to grow a wider range of plants than you expect.

Watering

Watering is the aspect of orchid growing that causes the most worry to beginners and experienced growers alike. The old maxim applies here: 'When in doubt, don't'. Far more orchids die from over-watering than underwatering. It is impossible to lay down any hard and fast rules as to when to water because so many variables apply – temperature, ventilation, pot size, compost and the state of growth of the plant are some of the more obvious ones. A plant in new compost needs more water than one in a compost that has started to break down and is less well aerated; likewise a plant in active growth uses more water than one that is resting. Small pots dry out more quickly than large ones; and mounted plants need to be watered – or at least sprayed – more frequently than plants in pots.

In winter, once a week or even once a fortnight may be enough for orchids in pots yet in summer they may require watering at least twice a week, perhaps every other day in a hot spell.

Water quality

There is no doubt about the importance of water quality. Epiphytic orchids are adapted to take in almost pure rainwater with very low levels of dissolved salts and nutrients. So water with a high proportion of mineral salts is not suitable for orchids. Many growers in areas where the mains water has a high percentage of dissolved salts use rainwater for watering; others use reverse osmosis units which are said to remove up to 98 per cent of dissolved salts. Hard water does not seem to be too harmful but an unsightly deposit of calcium salts builds up on leaves over time and can block the pores through which gas exchange takes place. If the water is highly chlorinated, leave it to stand overnight to remove most of the chlorine.

Water temperature

Whatever the source and quality of the water, it is important that it should be at air temperature rather than used straight from the mains. Watering with cold water causes black spots and blotching on leaves, which is unsightly in itself and may lead to fungal infection and bud drop. Sophisticated equipment is available, but it is simpler to have a water tank or drum in the greenhouse. Fill the tank each evening, allow it to stand overnight to warm up, then use the water the following day and refill the tank after you have finished. This system also helps to get rid of any excess chlorine in the water.

Watering cans are perfectly good for small collections of plants, but it is possible to rig up a pump and hose to take the hard work out of watering large collections. Use a submersible pump of the kind sold for fountains in ornamental ponds and connect it to a hose and watering lance. Place the pump in your water tank in the greenhouse so that it pumps the warmed water through the hose. Refill the tank from the mains after watering.

Feeding

Orchids have evolved to have low fertilizer requirements. In the wild, epiphytic orchids depend on minerals arising from the breakdown of bark, the occasional bird dropping and the very low amounts that have dissolved in rainwater, and almost all terrestrial orchids grow in areas with poor soil of low nutritional value. So any fertilizer must be applied in very dilute form. It is possible to buy fertilizers specially formulated for orchids and startling claims are made for many of these. However, ordinary houseplant fertilizers can be used as long as they are given at only a quarter to a half of the recommended strength.

Over time, bark is broken down by bacteria and these use up nitrogen. So orchids grown in bark-based composts need a high-nitrogen fertilizer. The source of the nitrogen should be nitrates, not urea, so check the composition given on the packet. Growers vary in how often they apply fertilizers; some go on the 'weakly, weekly' principle while others use a weak fertilizer solution for three waterings out of four. Whatever system is used and whatever the compost, it is important to flush the pots regularly with plain water to prevent any build-up of salts. Blackened root tips and black leaf tips are signs of too much fertilizer.

Types of fertilizer

The main elements supplied by a fertilizer are nitrogen, phosphorus and potassium and the composition is usually expressed in numbers shown on the packet – for example, 30:30:30 indicates a fertilizer with equal amounts of the three major nutrients. A high-nitrogen fertilizer will be shown as 30:10:10, while 10:10:30 indicates one that is high in potassium. Many growers use a high-nitrogen fertilizer in spring and early summer to promote growth, and change to a high-potassium mixture in late summer and autumn to give the next season's flowering a boost. One element that does not usually appear in fertilizers is calcium. In hard-water areas this is never in short supply but in soft-water areas, application of a weak solution of calcium nitrate is beneficial. Frequency of fertilizing should be reduced or even stopped altogether when orchids are not in active growth, which usually means in winter.

Light and shade

Orchids are often considered to be plants with high light requirements but few people who have not seen them growing in the wild realize in what deep shade some species grow. A few grow low down on tree trunks in dense forests, where a light meter gives no reading at all. More species grow higher up in the trees, usually on the larger branches, where there is a little more light, but very few grow right up in the canopy. Among the epiphytes, it is only really those that grow on rocks rather than trees that are used to more intense light. Even the terrestrial orchids that grow in the open, in bogs and grassland, often get some shade from grass.

Greenhouse variations

All greenhouses will have one area that is more shaded than another. If the greenhouse is aligned east to west, the staging running along the south side will be much brighter than that on the north side, which may be further shaded if there are plants hanging in the middle of the greenhouse. Orchids that like heavy shade can be hung below the staging, and so it is possible to accommodate most preferences.

It is not hard to tell by appearances if a plant is getting the right amount of light. If the shade is too heavy, it will have dark green and luxuriant foliage but may not flower, while if it is getting too much light it may flower well but have small, yellowish leaves.

Repotting

Repotting is necessary in three circumstances:

1
If a plant is obviously outgrowing its pot, then it should be moved to a larger pot with fresh compost. This is best done just as new roots are starting to develop; if they are too long, they are easily broken.

2
If the compost has broken down and has become denatured and soggy the plant should be repotted as soon as possible. If many of the roots have died, it can be repotted into the same size of pot or even a smaller one.

3
If a plant just seems to be sitting still, without making growth, then fresh compost often seems to give it a boost even though the original compost has retained its structure.

Sometimes even with plastic pots, roots cling to the inside of the pot and are difficult to detach without damage. In this case, soak the pot with its plant in a bucket of water for half an hour and usually the roots then come away quite easily. In all cases, dead roots should be cut away; they will be brown and feel soft when pressed lightly. Dead pseudo-bulbs can be removed at the same time. Do not be tempted to use too large a pot for repotting: an orchid should always be put into a pot which is only just big enough to accommodate its root system.

Well-grown orchids are, by and large, healthy plants but they can fall victim to any of the usual greenhouse pests, most of which also occur on houseplants. As in most things, prevention is better than cure and while it may be impossible to avoid an attack completely, the vigilant grower should be able to prevent a severe infestation. One simple rule is to keep the greenhouse as clean as possible and remove dead flowers and leaves regularly. While some pests, such as aphids, enter a greenhouse through open vents, most are introduced on other plants. Any new plant should be examined carefully before being introduced to a collection. Ideally, it should first go into a quarantine area but this is often not practical.

Pests and diseases

4

Pests and diseases

Controlling pests

Pests can be roughly divided into those that spend most of their life cycle on a plant, such as scale insects and red spider mite, and those that roam around seeking what they may devour, such as slugs, snails and woodlice. The latter group, although in general less serious, are often more difficult to deal with.

Biological control

Most greenhouse pests are themselves attacked by some kind of predator and these can sometimes be used by the grower to kill the pests. The big advantage of biological control is that it is very specific and only the pest is affected, not other insects which may be harmless or even beneficial. The main disadvantage is that the pests are never completely wiped out – it is not in the interest of a predator to kill off its food source entirely. A low level of infestation may not matter if the plants are grown purely for pleasure, but a professional grower cannot sell or show plants with damaged leaves. If biological control is being used it is not possible to use chemical methods at the same time. Several firms, which advertise in horticultural magazines, will supply the parasites and predators that are necessary.

Chemical control

As well as biological control, pests can also be controlled with chemical pesticides. Pesticides are either systemic or contact in their action. Systemic pesticides are taken up inside the plant and kill only pests that feed on that plant; other insects are unaffected. Contact pesticides are applied to the foliage of the plant; they are unselective and kill any pest that they touch but those that lurk in leaf axils, for example, may escape unharmed.

It might, then, seem obvious that systemic pesticides are preferable but they do not work in all cases. Scale insects, for example, do not take in enough plant sap to kill them.

All garden centres carry a good selection of pesticides. If you choose to use them, follow the instructions on the packet exactly, including the safety instructions. It goes without saying that you should always make sure that a chemical is recommended against the pest in question.

Spider mites

Red spider mite and false spider mite are probably the most serious pests of orchids because they are the most insidious. The creatures themselves are so small that they are difficult to see and usually the first warning is the silvery appearance of a plant's leaves, particularly the underside, which later turn brown. Red spider mite is often said to be more prevalent in dry conditions but it can still flourish when the humidity is high. In winter, when the day length is less than 12 hours, the mites may migrate to the frame of the greenhouse and hibernate within webs. So, if possible, wash the frame with dilute bleach at this time of year to help stop any build-up.

There is a predatory mite that provides a well-established means of biological control against spider mites.

It should be introduced when red spider mite numbers are rising, that is in spring. It attacks all stages of the mite's life cycle – egg, nymph and adult. If chemical control is preferred, the insecticide has to be changed every few years as the mites develop resistance to chemicals. The eggs are immune to virtually all insecticides and so applications should be repeated after ten days by which time the eggs will have hatched.

False spider mite can also attack orchids and is susceptible to the same pesticides as red spider mite. It is particularly serious on pleiones, where it hides under the pseudobulbs and thus escapes contact with the pesticide. To deal with this problem, lift the pleiones, spray with the relevant pesticide and repot into fresh compost and clean pots.

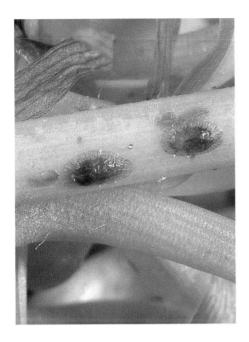

Scale insects

Several kinds of scale insects can affect orchids and all have a hardened, waxy shield which covers and protects the insect. They look rather like miniature limpets and, although small, are easy to see, unlike red spider mites. The waxy shield repels water and so insecticides carried in water are ineffective. Wiping the affected area with methylated spirit (known as rubbing alcohol in America) can clear a small infestation; a small brush or a cotton wool bud makes a good applicator. For larger infestations, white oil, malathion, dimethoate and diazinon are effective. Orchids often share a greenhouse with other plants, for example ferns, which are also susceptible to scale and these, too, must be checked. Adult scale insects do not move around, but newly hatched nymphs are mobile and can colonize a new area.

Mealy bugs

These insects belong to the same family as scale insects and are easily seen as they are covered by a white, waxy coating. They can be controlled by the same insecticides as scale insects, but biological control is also an option: a species of ladybird is available which is an effective predator but it needs a relatively high and stable temperature to succeed, around 21°C (70°F)

Aphids

All gardeners are familiar with aphids; greenfly and blackfly are facts of horticultural life. Although orchids are less susceptible than many plants, aphids are attracted by new growth and particularly by flower buds. Both young leaves and flowers can become badly distorted but the most serious aspect of aphid infestation is that they are important carriers of viruses. Most insecticides kill aphids but it should be possible to spot them when there are only a few, when they can easily be wiped off. However, they multiply quickly so the grower must be vigilant.

Vine weevils

Vine weevils, which seem to be on the increase, cause damage in two ways. The adults eat circular holes in leaves and the grubs, which are white with a brown head and are about 8mm (⅜in) long, live below the soil surface and feed on roots and tubers. The damage caused by adults is unlikely to be fatal but it is unsightly and long lasting. It is the grubs, however, that pose the biggest risk. You are unlikely to find grubs in a bark-based compound and they would certainly not like rockwool, but terrestrial orchids growing in a peat-based compost could be at risk.

The grubs can be killed by the insecticide Sybol, but biological control is also possible in the form of a parasitic nematode (a type of eel worm), which attacks both adults and larvae. Adults can enter a greenhouse through open vents and one way of controlling them is to use an insectocutor, an electrical insect killer, although it will kill any flying insect that is attracted to light. Vine weevils are very cryptic and emerge only at night. It is said that if one goes into a greenhouse after dark, any vine weevils there can be traced by the sound of crunching jaws.

Woodlice

Woodlice feed mainly on decaying veg-
etable matter and many people believe
that they do no harm to living plants,
but they definitely eat the growing tips
of orchid roots. They lurk under pots that
are standing on a solid surface and you
may occasionally find one in a pot when
repotting. They probably do most damage to mounted orchids where they can
hide under the plant or on the back of
a mount, so it is always worth checking
the backs of mounted plants from time
to time. Woodlice are susceptible to
almost any insecticide.

Slugs and snails

These are the bane of every gardener.
If a greenhouse has a concrete base,
that helps to prevent the entry of slugs
but some always find their way inside
where they live in and under pots and
forage at night. The presence of chewed
leaves and flower buds, and a trail of
slime gives away their presence. They
also climb and are just as likely to
damage mounted plants. Slug pellets
scattered around pots where slime trails
are visible should be effective, and a
saucer of beer on the greenhouse floor
usually claims some victims. Frogs and
toads, which often take up residence in
a greenhouse, offer useful biological
control. Another form is a nematode that
lives off slugs, but there is unlikely to be
a big enough population of slugs inside a
greenhouse for this to be very practical.

Garlic snails

Garlic snails are tiny snails with a flat shell, about 5mm (¼in) in diameter, which are often found in orchid houses, being passed around between growers on pots and plants. They tend to live in the pots during the day and emerge in the evening. They do not seem to be affected by slug pellets, but reasonable control can be achieved by walking round the orchid house in the evening and crushing any that are seen. When crushed they smell of garlic, hence the name. At least growers in temperate climates are spared the depredations of the giant African snail, which grows to 15cm (6in) long and can demolish an orchid in a single day.

Preventing diseases

Not many fungal diseases are specific to orchids but leaf spotting caused by fungus is common. It usually occurs when a plant has been over-watered, particularly when the temperature is low and there is poor ventilation. Bacterial rot can set in if water lies for too long in leaf joints, and terrestrial orchids succumb very readily to stem rot if the compost is too wet while they are not in active growth.

Once again, prevention is better than cure. Watering should be carried out early enough in the day for leaves to be dry by nightfall when the temperature falls and the relative humidity rises. In the wild, of course, rain often falls at night but conditions there are very different from those in an enclosed glasshouse. In cases of fungal spotting, remove damaged leaves and spray the plant with a fungicide. With bacterial rot, it is usually too late to save the plant by the time it becomes evident; but in epiphytic orchids, if the stem and roots are firm, the plant may branch from lower down the stem. Any damaged tissue should be removed and the area treated with Physan or dusted with sulphur powder.

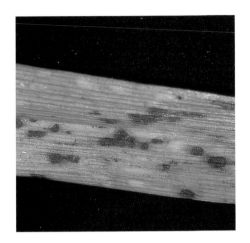

Viruses

Several viruses occur in orchids, the most common being cymbidium mosaic virus, which does not affect only cymbidiums although it is more common on them. The symptoms of viral infection are irregular, pale patches on young leaves that eventually turn brown or black, or sometimes yellow streaks on a leaf. At present there is no cure for viruses and an affected plant should be discarded before it affects others. Viruses can be transmitted from plant to plant in several ways; for example, by using a knife contaminated with sap from an affected plant to propagate an unaffected one, or by repotting into an affected pot. Obviously cleanliness is important; knives and scissors should be dipped in disinfectant before they are used, but it is not enough as one of the most common causes of virus spread is by sucking insects such as aphids.

Physiological damage

Not all marks found on an orchid's leaves are caused by infection or insect damage. Cold water on a leaf surface can cause black spotting, particularly on young leaves. This can be avoided by using water that is already at the temperature of the greenhouse and spraying only when the temperature is high.

Heat can cause damage as well as cold. Sunlight on a leaf can scorch it, particularly if the leaf is wet; unfortunately such marks are likely to remain on a plant for at least two years, until the leaf is finally shed. Yellow leaves may be caused by too much light or by mineral deficiencies – in the latter case the yellow is usually rather blotchy, whereas in the former the leaves will be an even yellow green. If you suspect a mineral deficiency, sprinkle a teaspoon of magnesium sulphate (Epsom salts) or iron sequestrene on the surface of the potting medium and water it in. Both are available in garden centres.

Blackening and dying of leaf tips is often the result of too strong a fertilizer or a build-up of salts in the compost. The best treatment is to repot the plant and make sure the circumstances do not arise again. Trim off the black tips; it does not usually spread but the plants look better for it.

Sometimes the new leaves on a plant appear as though they have been folded horizontally, as if to make a fan. This seems to be particularly prevalent in *Miltoniopsis* hybrids. This is caused by too dry a compost; if water is applied, the rest of the leaf should be smooth but the folded part remains, a permanent reminder of the owner's oversight.

All orchid growers want to increase their plants at some time and orchids, like other plants, can be propagated either vegetatively or from seed. For the average grower, the former is by far the most practical method.

Propagation

5

Propagation

Vegetative propagation

Vegetative propagation involves increasing a plant by division or from cuttings and results in two or more identical plants.

Sympodial orchids

Sympodial orchids are easily divided; they produce new growths every year and sometimes more or less divide themselves when the old, central growth dies. Division is best carried out when new roots are starting to develop on the new growths; if the roots are allowed to grow too long they can be difficult to fit into a pot and are more likely to break. Usually the leafy part of the growth and the roots develop together but in some plants the leafy growth may be fully formed before roots start to appear and then it is necessary to wait until the roots are growing before the plant is divided. The rhizome (creeping stem) is cut between two pseudobulbs or growths with a sharp, sterile knife or secateurs and the two (or more) parts are then potted up in the usual way. Do not be tempted to divide small plants, however; a division should have at least three pseudobulbs and preferably more.

Above: The rhizome is cut with a sharp, sterile knife.

Below: The two parts of the plant are carefully eased apart.

Above: The old roots
are trimmed with sterile
secateurs.

Below: The two halves of
the original plant are now
ready for potting.

Back bulbs

Some orchids, such as cymbidiums, can be propagated from leafless back bulbs. Choose an old pseudobulb, cut it off at its base, and clean it up by removing any loose sheaths. Allow the cut edge to dry for a couple of days to lessen the risk of infection and then plant it to about a third of its height in perlite, grit or sharp sand and keep it cool and moist. A new shoot should appear within three months and once it has developed its own roots, which could take another two to three months, pot it up in standard compost. Another method is to put the back bulb in a polythene bag along with some damp sphagnum moss, seal the bag and hang it up in a warm, shady place. Leave it, as before, for two to three months until a shoot develops.

Monopodial orchids

Monopodial orchids are less easy to divide, but if the stems branch and the branches form their own roots, detach them and pot up as new plants. Vandas tend to develop long stems and become straggly. In almost all cases, the upper part of the stem has roots and if it is cut below some roots, the top part can be removed and treated as a new plant. The basal part will usually branch out and grow again.

Monopodial orchids can be divided by cutting the stem between roots.

Keikis

Some orchids, both sympodial and monopodial, develop 'keikis' - this is a Hawaiian word meaning babies. These are small plants that grow from dormant buds on a pseudobulb or a flower spike. Many species of *Dendrobium* and *Epidendrum* develop keikis on their pseudobulbs, and some other orchids, such as *Phalaenopsis* and *Aeranthes*, occasionally produce them on the flower spikes. Once these little plants have developed a few short roots, they can be cut away with a sharp, sterile knife and potted up separately. The roots develop quickly and it is important to catch them before they grow too long and brittle.

Cuttings

Cuttings differ from divisions in that they do not have roots when they are removed from the parent plant. All gardeners are used to taking cuttings and there are a few orchids that will grow well from cuttings. Species of *Vanilla* can be increased in this way, as can some species of *Angraecum* such as *Angraecum distichum*. These cuttings produce roots much more readily in perlite than in bark and a heated propagator will speed things up greatly. Stems of many species of *Dendrobium* and *Epidendrum* can be cut into sections and either laid on a tray of damp moss or planted in perlite or grit. In this way, they will often produce new shoots provided a dormant bud is present. Any cuttings should be taken when the plants are growing actively, which will usually be in spring or summer.

Meristem propagation

Any method of vegetative propagation results in identical offspring, while propagation by seed does not. For this reason, a particular hybrid must be increased vegetatively rather than from seed, as seedlings are always variable. However, while taking cuttings and dividing plants are satisfactory methods for an amateur grower or small nursery, it takes a long time to build up a sizeable stock in this way. This is one reason why, in the past, particularly desirable forms of orchids were so expensive. In the past 30 years, however, the technique of meristem culture (a type of tissue culture) has been developed. This results in thousands of identical plants that can be grown on quickly and sold cheaply and is the source of most of the orchids sold in supermarkets and garden centres. The technique must be carried out in sterile conditions and while it is theoretically straightforward, few if any amateur growers attempt it.

Orchid seedlings growing in a community pot.

Growing from seed

Almost all orchids are insect pollinated and they are often adapted for pollination by only one species of insect. These adaptations vary from something simple like a nectar-filled spur to such bizarre modifications as mimicry, when a flower resembles a female insect and emits a scent resembling the insect's pheromones to attract a male. In the absence of the right insect, we must pollinate a plant ourselves and so long as the orchid has flowers of a reasonable size, this is not too difficult.

The diagrams overleaf show the position of the anther and the stigma in a typical orchid flower. The pollinia, or pollen clumps, which lie under the anther cap, are easily lifted off using a cocktail stick and they should then be placed on the stigma of the same or another flower. The receptive surface of the stigma is sticky and there is rarely a problem in getting the pollinia to adhere to it. It is usually obvious within a few days whether the pollination has worked or not, as the flower starts to go over and the ovary (the part immediately below the flower) shows signs of swelling.

If the aim is to produce seed of a species, it is always best to pollinate the flower of another plant of the same species. Of course this may not be possible and it is always worth trying to self-pollinate a flower if you have only one plant of that species. Some species seem to be self-sterile but more often than not the pollination will succeed, although the resulting seedlings may be fewer in number and less vigorous than

Structure of Cypripedium calceolus

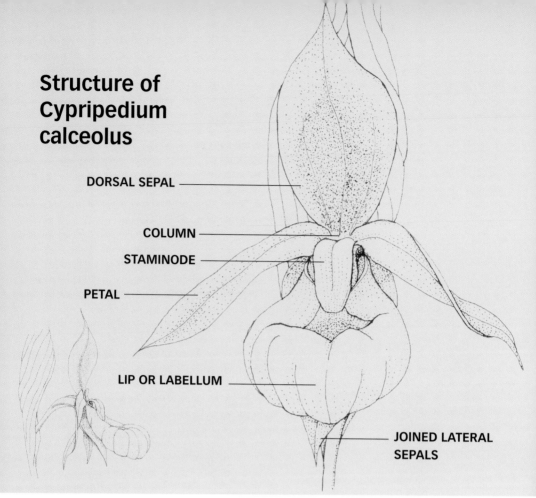

DORSAL SEPAL

COLUMN

STAMINODE

PETAL

LIP OR LABELLUM

JOINED LATERAL SEPALS

Structure of Aerangis luteo–alba

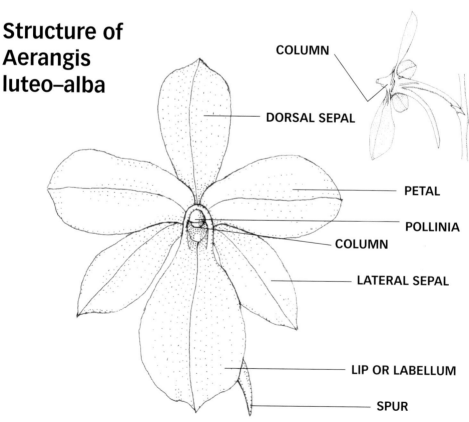

COLUMN

DORSAL SEPAL

PETAL

POLLINIA

COLUMN

LATERAL SEPAL

LIP OR LABELLUM

SPUR

when two plants are involved. In hybridization, two plants of different species or different hybrids are involved, but the method of pollination is the same. It is important to keep records from which to label and judge the resulting offspring; any developing seed pods should be labelled while still on the plant, giving the names of the plants involved and the date on which the cross was made.

Harvesting the seed

The length of time an orchid seed pod takes to develop varies enormously, from two months to over a year. As a general rule, the larger the seed pod, the longer it takes but there are plenty of exceptions. Usually, when a pod is starting to ripen, it begins to change colour from green to yellowish or pinkish. When this happens, it is a good idea to remove it from the plant, wrap it loosely in tissue paper and leave it in a warm, dry place until it splits. Then shake out the seed and remove any pieces of pod; these are difficult to sterilize and may act as a focus for infection when the seed comes to be sown.

Seed keeps for a considerable time if it is dry; the easiest way to store it is to keep it in a screw-top jar in a refrigerator with silica gel or some other desiccant in the bottom of the jar.

Orchid seed can also be sown from an unripe seed pod. This is known as 'green podding'. An advantage of this method is that the seed itself does not need to be sterilized, only the outside of the capsule. The capsule should be full size, but not yet ripe; only experience will tell when this has occurred. If capsules, either green or almost ripe, are to be sent through the post it is essential that they are packed in a rigid container so that they do not get crushed. Even ripe seed should be wrapped in something like bubble plastic to give it some protection.

Orchid seed

Orchids produce vast amounts of tiny seeds. The seeds are so small because they do not contain the food reserves found in almost all other seeds. They therefore need a fungus, which may be present in soil or on the bark of a tree, to provide food for growth. Orchid seed can be carried on the wind for great distances and the likelihood of coming across the correct fungus is not high, but so many seeds are produced by one plant that the chances are increased.

Early attempts at seed sowing

In the early days of orchid growing, attempts were made to grow orchids from seed. These were met with little success, until it was found that if the seed was sown around the base of the parent plant, some might germinate and grow on. At the end of the 19th century, Noel Bernard, a French botanist, discovered that orchid seeds were dependent on a fungus for germination and growth. But it was not until the 1920s that Lewis Knudson, an American, discovered that the nutrients provided by the fungus in the wild could be provided artificially by the sower. He experimented with various chemical solutions containing mineral salts and sugars that he added to agar jelly, a substance derived from seaweed. This is the basis of methods used today. As such a nutrient solution is also ideal for the growth of bacteria and fungi, everything, including the seed itself, must be sterilized.

Orchid seedlings in a flask.

Sowing orchid seed

Because of the need for sterile conditions, growing orchids from seed is easier in a laboratory using specially designed equipment, but it can be done successfully using more basic materials such as a pressure cooker and a sterile box or aquarium tank. It is possible to buy nutrient agar so there is no need to make up complicated chemical solutions. The seed is sown into the agar jelly in a glass flask, then the flasks are sealed and kept at a warm, even temperature. Provided all has been kept sterile and the flask is not invaded by fungi or bacteria, you should see signs of the seed developing into what are known as protocorms within a couple of weeks. Protocorms look like lumps of green tissue and they soon develop into tiny plants. As the seedlings grow, they must be replated, that is transferred to a new flask with a fresh and slightly stronger nutrient solution, and grown on again. This also must be done in sterile conditions. There is no space here to go into the methods used in detail; anyone who would like to know more should refer to a book on the subject.

Deflasking

Not many amateur growers attempt to grow orchids from seed themselves, but sooner or later, most find themselves buying orchid seedlings in flasks. For anyone with patience, this is by far the cheapest way to build up a collection. A further advantage is that seedlings in flasks do not need to have CITES permits and plant health certificates, both of which are required when importing mature plants from abroad.

Seedlings grow more quickly in a flask than in a pot and so, in theory, it is a good idea to leave them in the flask as long as possible. However, commercial flasks prepared for sale to the public often have only a thin layer of agar in the bottom and if this has dried up, or if it is filled with roots, then action has to be taken quickly. Likewise, if there are lots of yellow leaves or the seedlings have stopped growing, then it is also time to deflask.

First of all, prepare some pots. Fill some clean plastic pots with a mixture of fine orchid bark and perlite; it is a good idea to put a couple of polystyrene chips in the bottom of the pot to improve the drainage. Stand the bark-filled pots in a sink and pour boiling water over them; this has some sterilizing effect and also washes out most of the fine dust from the bark and perlite. Leave the pots to cool.

Flasks come in many shapes and sizes. Wide-mouthed screw-top jars are frequently used and these are easy to deal with. Prepare a bowl of warm water, open the flask and gently ease the seedlings out into the water. Wash off any agar clinging to the roots; handle the seedlings carefully as leaves and roots break off with alarming ease.

Spread the little plants out on absorbent paper and let them dry off slightly.

Sometimes flasks are bottles of various kinds, and these have to be broken before the seedlings can be extracted. The simplest way is to wrap the bottle in a towel and hit it with a hammer, using just enough force to break the glass but not enough to squash the seedlings inside. Then, wearing gloves, open the towel, pick off the pieces of broken glass and treat the seedlings as before.

We now have seedlings, often with long tangled roots, lying on a piece of absorbent paper. At this point they can be sprayed with a dilute solution of a fungicide/bactericide such as Physan. This is not essential, but it helps to protect the still vulnerable seedlings from infection. The young roots that have grown into the agar never (or hardly ever) turn into adult roots; these grow later from the base of the stem. So the young roots should be trimmed with sterile scissors as otherwise they rot easily, forming a focus for infection, and may also interfere with the growth of the adult roots. Trim the roots down to 2–3 cm (1in) in length, removing any that are very thin or that coil up under the plant.

Community pots

Often the seedlings will be mixed in size and they should be sorted out into more or less matching groups. Plant as many seedlings from each group as possible into one pot because they grow better close together in the early stages. This is known as a community pot.

Now the seedlings must be hardened off before they go into the greenhouse to gradually get them used to the change in climate. A propagator is useful here; they are available in a variety of sizes and most have vents in the lid that can be closed to start with, then opened gradually. Failing that, the community pot can be put into a polythene bag which is sealed at first and then gradually opened to let in air. Results are likely to be much better if seedlings are deflasked in spring or summer, when they grow on quickly.

Seedlings can be left in the community pots for quite a long time. It is usually obvious when they need to be moved on. Either they start to climb out of the pots, with roots waving in the air and finding their way into other pots, or else they stop growing and need the boost that repotting often gives. When they come out of the community pots, they can either be mounted on a bark slab or potted individually. With luck, you will not have to wait too long to see them flower.

While most orchids now in cultivation are artificially bred hybrids, up until the second half of the 19th century only naturally occurring species were grown, which were collected from the wild. The earliest hybrid orchid known to flower was a cross between *Calanthe furcata* and *Calanthe masuca* made by John Dominy, the foreman of the famous orchid nursery Veitch & Sons. He collected seed from this cross in 1854 and a young plant flowered only two years later; it was named *Calanthe* Dominyi. This was not John Dominy's first successful attempt at hybridization; that took place a year earlier and was a cross between two species of *Cattleya*, believed to be *Cattleya guttata* and *Cattleya loddigesii*, but the plants from this cross took six years to flower.

Hybridization

Hybridization

Registration of hybrids

By the end of the 19th century a great many hybrids had been made and had flowered. After 1871, new hybrids were published in the *Gardener's Chronicle*, and from 1893, also in the *Orchid Review* which was established that year.

In 1895 the orchid firm Sander & Sons of St Albans, England, began to register orchid hybrids and in 1906, the first *Sander's List of Orchid Hybrids* was published. Additional volumes appeared at intervals of some years until 1961, when the Royal Horticultural Society became the International Registration Authority. *Sander's List of Orchid Hybrids* is still used today and now the list, containing almost 100,000 names, is available both in print and on compact disc.

Complex hybrids and their names

The first orchid hybrids were between two species of the same genus but it was not long before the first intergeneric cross (between two different genera) was made. This was in 1863, between *Cattleya mossiae* and *Laelia crispa*, to give *Laeliocattleya* Exoniensis. In 1886, *Sophrocattleya* Batemaniana was the result of a cross between *Sophronitis grandiflora* and *Cattleya intermedia*, and in 1892 the first trigeneric hybrid was made: *Sophrolaeliocattleya* Veitchiana, the result of crossing *Sophronitis grandiflora* with *Laeliocattleya* Schilleriana.

So far, the names of intergeneric hybrids had been made by amalgamating the names of the genera involved but as crosses became more complex, involving four or more genera, it became obvious that another way of naming must be found. It was proposed that in these circumstances, the suffix 'ara' should be added to the name of someone who was involved in either growing or studying orchids.

Among the earliest of such names is *Vuylstekeara* (*Cochlioda* x *Miltonia* x *Odontoglossum*) which was registered in 1911; C. Vuylsteke was a Belgian orchid grower and hybridizer. *Potinara* (*Brassavola* x *Cattleya* x *Laelia* x *Sophronitis*), registered in 1922, is another early name, after M. Potin, a French grower.

These 'manufactured' generic names are written like other generic names in italics and start with a capital letter. The result of a cross between any two species or hybrids is known as a 'grex'. For example, all plants resulting from a cross between *Sophronitis grandiflora* and *Cattleya intermedia* must be called *Sophrocattleya* Batemaniana, regardless of which is the pollen parent and which the seed parent, which varieties were used or when the cross was made. The progeny may look very different and particular forms can be given a cultivar name. Grex names and cultivar names are both written in plain type (not italics) and begin with a capital letter, but the cultivar name is enclosed in single quotation marks; for example, *Vuylstekeara* Cambria 'Plush'. Any awarded plant, whether a species or a hybrid, must be given a cultivar name.

Doing it yourself

Many growers eventually feel the urge to create their own hybrids. Pollination is done in the same way as described in Chapter 5, but if it is to be an intergeneric cross, the genera must be compatible. This usually means that they must be closely related; for example, it is easy to cross *Cattleya* and *Laelia*, but not *Cattleya* with *Cymbidium*. Even so, several attempts may be necessary before the cross is successful.

If you wish to make a serious attempt at hybridization, it is important to have some goal in mind rather than just crossing two plants that happen to be in flower at the same time. The aim might be the production of larger flowers on a more compact plant, for example, or a particular colour of flower. It is necessary to have the space, and patience, to grow many seedlings from the cross on to flowering size – the smallest and slowest might just be the one to have the desired characteristics.

Much is now known about the compatibility of different genera and the inheritance of various characteristics and it is worth reading as much as possible about this before you begin. There is no point wasting years learning from your own mistakes when you could learn very quickly from those of others.

Why grow hybrids?

More people grow hybrid orchids than species. As there are estimated to be over 100,000 registered hybrids with the numbers rising every year, there is plenty of choice. What advantages do hybrids have over species?

The first advantage, not confined to orchids, is what is known as 'hybrid vigour'. Two rather temperamental species can, when crossed, produce a vigorous and easily grown hybrid. As well as growing more quickly, hybrids often flower earlier and more freely and are more tolerant of less than ideal conditions. A grower may want a particular flower colour on a certain size of plant that will grow well in the conditions on offer. It may be difficult to find these characteristics in a species (in fact such a plant may not exist) but it is very likely that there will be a hybrid to fit the bill.

Also, at a more basic level, hybrids are cheaper and more readily available. Like everything else, however, orchids are affected by fashion and this is reflected in the price. The genera which are currently the most popular can be seen by looking at the pages of new registrations which are printed in the *Orchid Review*. Most growers cultivate both hybrids and species although they tend to favour one more than the other. It is perhaps fortunate that there are enough species enthusiasts to keep the raw material for hybrids alive.

Dict. Icon. des Orch.

Calanthe, hybr. pl.2.

A. Goossens, pinx.

Lith. J.L.Goffart, Bruxelles.

CALANTHE DOMINII, Ldl

Calanthe Dominyi was the
first man-made hybrid orchid
to flower.

Two of the most frequently grown
and easily available orchids are
suited to cool conditions; these are
cymbidiums and odontoglossums
and their hybrids.

Orchids for
the cool greenhouse
minimum night-time temperature **10°C (50°F)**

7

Orchids for the cool greenhouse

Cymbidium

Probably more growers start with a *Cymbidium* than any other type of orchid, as they are widely available and do well as houseplants. There are about 50 species that occur in Asia and Australia but the hybrids are far more widely grown. Cymbidiums need a free-draining compost, usually based on medium bark, and do well in large plastic pots. They are usually bought in flower and although they are easy to grow, it is not always easy to get them to flower the following year. During the summer, they require copious watering and feeding to build up large pseudobulbs. They also need a marked contrast between day and night temperatures – they will not flower without cool nights. The night-time temperature should be about 10°C (50°F) in autumn, winter and spring. It can fall as low as 6°C (43°F) without any harm being done; however, if the night-time temperature rises above about 15°C (59°F), flower buds may drop. In winter, a daytime temperature of 15–18°C (60–65°F) is sufficient; in summer it can rise much higher but the plants will suffer if the temperature is over 30°C (86°F).

Plants benefit from being outside in summer in a bright situation, sheltered from the wind and not exposed to direct sunlight, which can scorch leaves. In winter, they should only be given enough water to prevent the pseudobulbs from shrivelling. Flower stems should be staked soon after they start to develop. Plants should be repotted when the new growths become pressed against the side of the pot. This is best done after flowering or in early spring and they can be divided at the same time. Most need dividing every two to three years.

Dwarf species.

Dwarf *Cymbidium* species have been grown for centuries in China and Japan where their grassy leaves and small, elegant flowers are much appreciated. Special ceramic pots are often used for their cultivation. Some are almost hardy.

C. devonianum
is a species from the Himalayas with pendent flower spikes bearing green flowers heavily marked with purple-red; the lip is pink, spotted with red.

C. erythrostylum,
from Vietnam, has arching flower spikes in spring and summer of up to seven white flowers with a bright yellow lip striped with red.

C. floribundum,
from China and Japan, flowers in spring with erect or arching spikes of many greenish-yellow flowers marked with red or brown. The lip is white with red marks.

C. tigrinum
is a Burmese species with honey-scented green or yellow flowers faintly marked with purple or red and a white lip with purple bars.

Cymbidium 'Bernard Buttercup'

Standard hybrids

These grow into large plants and take up a lot of space, but their spectacular flowers last for up to two months. They are popular as cut flowers and are available in almost every colour except blue. Most flower in late winter and spring. There are hundreds of varieties; there is no space here to mention more than a few.

Caithness 'Cooksbridge', FCC/RHS large, pale green flowers.

Cariga 'Tetra Canary', AM/RHS yellow flower with purple-red marks on the lip.

Coraki 'Red Pauwels' orange-yellow flowers.

Dingwall 'Lewes' white flowers with red-marked lips.

Fort George 'Lewes' , AM/RHS green flowers with purple on the lip; very free flowering.

Howick 'Cooksbridge', AM/RHS large white flowers with a crimson lip.

Many Waters 'Stonehurst', AM/RHS yellow flowers.

Valley Courtier yellow flowers.

Via Abril Roja 'Rose' pink flowers.

Miniature Hybrids

These are mainly derived from the dwarf species described above. They make good houseplants and some have scented flowers. Many have green, yellow or brownish flowers, often with dark marks on the lip, but the range of colours is increasing all the time.

Bulbarrow 'Our Midge' rose red flowers with a darker lip.

Cherry Blossom 'Profusion' only 30cm (12in) tall; pink flowers with darker spots.

Peter Pan 'Greensleeves' scented, green flowers with a crimson lip; autumn flowering.

Stonehaven 'Cooksbridge' cream flowers with yellow and red lip; flowers autumn/winter.

Strathaven usually pink flowers.

Touchstone 'Janis' bronze flowers with a crimson lip.

Hybrids of *C. tigrinum* are mostly green or yellow and appear in spring. They include Wood Nymph, Tiger Cub and Tiger Tail.

Miniature cymbidium Petit Port 'Mont Millais'

Novelty Hybrids

Some of the best modern hybrids result from a cross between miniature and standard hybrids and are often called novelty or intermediate hybrids – the flowers are as large as those of the standards but the plants are smaller.
Bunny Girl 'Lily White' white flowers, faintly tinged with green.
Calle de Mar 'Green Beauty' green flowers with a crimson lip.
Ivy Fung 'Radiance' mahogany red flowers, edged with cream.
Rincon Fairy 'Pink Perfection' deep pink flowers with red-spotted lips.

Odontoglossum

Most of the 60 species of *Odontoglossum* come from the mountainous areas of Central and South America and so prefer cool temperatures. Grow in a free-draining bark compost with good ventilation and feed and water freely in the growing season. The roots should not remain dry for long periods. They make good houseplants and are slightly unusual in that they tend not to flower at the same time each year but on a nine to ten month cycle, after the new pseudobulb has fully developed.

O. crispum

is a beautiful species from Colombia with many-flowered, arching spikes up to 50cm (20in) long. The flowers have frilly edges, are up to 10cm (4in) in diameter, and are white, often flushed with pink. The lip is marked with yellow and red. There are many awarded clones .

O. harryanum

is another Colombian species with branched flower spikes to 1m (3ft)

Odontoglossum Violetta von Holme

tall. The flowers grow to 10cm (4in) in diameter; the sepals and petals are yellow, heavily blotched with red-brown, the lip is white with red at its base.

O. odoratum,

from Venezuela, has a flower spike up to 75cm (30in) tall; the scented flowers are about 6cm (21/2in) in diameter, usually yellow spotted with red or brown.

Hybrids

As with *Cymbidium*, the hybrids are more widely grown than the species. *Odontoglossum* belongs to what is known as the Oncidium group of orchids, members of which breed easily with each other, so there are many complex crosses.

Odontoglossum Marie Kaino

Beallara
(Brassia x Cochlioda x Miltonia x Odontoglossum)
Tahoma Glacier 'Green' a vigorous plant with starry greenish-white flowers with purplish marks on the petals and lip.

Burrageara
(Cochlioda x Miltonia x Odontoglossum x Oncidium)
Living Fire 'Redman' bright red.
Stefan Isler bright red with an orange lip.

Maclellanara
(Brassia x Odontoglossum x Oncidium)
Pagan Lovesong tall spikes of cream or

yellow-green flowers with large, brown spots. There are many awarded clones.
Hans Ruedi Isler striking yellow and brown flowers with a red-brown lip.

Odontioda
(Cochlioda x Odontoglossum)
This is the earliest of the crosses between two genera in the Oncidium group, first registered in 1904. Many are predominantly bright red.
Archirondel white flowers with a large maroon blotch on each segment, yellow in the centre.
City of Birmingham yellow flowers with purple and brown marks.
Eric Young large white flowers marked with red.
Heatoniensis star-shaped flowers in pale pink with red spots and a white lip; yellow in the centre. This is one of the earliest crosses.
Honiton Lace 'Burnham', AM/RHS mauve and pink flowers.
Ingmar orange-red flowers; the sepals and petals are tipped with lilac.
Keighleyensis small, star-shaped, bright red flowers.
Red Rum bright red flowers.
Trixon bright red flowers; the sepals and lip are tinged with lilac, and the lip has a yellow crest.

Odontocidium
(Odontoglossum x Oncidium)
The flower spikes are simple or branched, the flowers varied. Some are rounded, while others have long narrow sepals and petals. The flowers are often boldly marked and the lip can be large or small. Purbeck Gold, Summer Gold, Tiger Butter and Tiger Sun are all yellow with brown markings.

Vuylstekeara Cambria Plush

Odontonia
(Miltonia x Odontoglossum)
An early cross, registered in 1905. Many, but not all, are pastel coloured.
Berlioz 'Lecoufle' large white flowers flushed with mauve-pink, with purple marks radiating from the centre. Several other clones have received awards.
Boussole 'Blanche' pure white flowers with two maroon spots in the centre; free flowering.
Debutante 'Oxbow' brown and yellow flowers with a red and white lip.
Diane bright yellow flowers with brown spots on the sepals and lip; several awarded clones.
Molière very large white flowers sometimes flushed with pink, edged with mauve and with purple marks on the sepals and petals; several awarded clones.

Stewartara
(Ada x Cochlioda x Odontoglossum)
Joyce elegant sprays of bright brown and orange flowers.

Vuylstekeara
(Cochlioda x Miltonia x Odontoglossum)
The flower spikes are simple or branched, the flowers often multi-coloured.
Cambria 'Plush', FCC/RHS the sepals and petals are crimson, the lip white speckled with crimson, with a yellow crest. Said to be the most widely grown orchid in the world.
Jersey basically white flowers, but almost covered with maroon spots; the lip has a yellow crest.

Wilsonara
(Cochlioda x Odontoglossum x Oncidium)
The flower spikes are simple or branched. The flowers are varied but usually rounded in shape and often multicoloured.
Gold Moselle branched sprays of smallish, bright yellow flowers heavily spotted with red-brown.
Kolibri tall, branched sprays of small pink and purple flowers.
Tiger Talk chestnut brown sepals and petals and a golden lip, all tipped with cream.
Widecombe Fair large, branched sprays of small white flowers with purple spots.

Cochlioda

Cochlioda is related to *Oncidium* and *Odontoglossum* and comes from the Andes of Peru, Ecuador and Bolivia. They are small plants with round pseudobulbs, flattened from side to side, with one or two leaves. Grow them in pots with a free-draining compost, with high humidity at cool temperatures. Some species have been used in crosses with *Oncidium* and *Odontoglossum*, where they add red to the colour range. There are six species, but only two are common in cultivation.

C. noezliana
has orange-red flowers 5cm (2in) in diameter, with a yellow callus on the lip and a violet column. It flowers in winter and spring.

C. rosea
has rosy red flowers 3cm (1in) in diameter, with a white callus on the lip, in winter.

Cochlioda rosea

Coelogyne

This large genus of over 100 species from tropical Asia includes several popular, easily grown and free-flowering species. The pseudobulbs are of various shapes and sizes, often large, set close together or well spaced on a woody rhizome. They have one or two leaves and one or many flowers on erect or pendent spikes. Grow in pots or baskets in a fairly coarse bark compost. Those that have pendent flower spikes will need to be hung up while in flower. Water freely while the plants are in active growth but keep almost dry when resting, providing just enough water to keep the pseudobulbs from shrivelling. Most species like good light.

C. cristata
is a popular and rewarding species from the Himalayas with large, round pseudobulbs and pendent spikes of up to ten white flowers with a yellow or orange blotch on the lip, up to 8cm (3in) in diameter. Winter to spring flowers.

C. dayana
is a striking species from Borneo with long, pendent spikes of cream and brown flowers in spring and summer.

C. fimbriata
has short spikes of one to three pale yellow flowers with a fringed lip.

C. massangeana,
with pale yellow and brown flowers, is similar to *C. dayana*.

C. mooreana
is a species from Vietnam with an erect spike of large white flowers with an orange blotch on the lip.

C. nitida
(synonym *C. ochracea*) is a compact, pretty species with erect spikes

of scented white flowers with yellow markings on the lip.

C. ovalis

has beige flowers in autumn; the lip has brownish marks and a fringed margin. This species grows easily and quickly but as the pseudobulbs are set well apart, it tends to climb out of a pot so is better in a basket.

Cypripedium

The temperate slipper orchids are terrestrial plants with deciduous, pleated leaves. The flower structure is similar to that of the tropical slipper orchids, with the lip forming the characteristic pouch. In *Cypripedium*, the edges of the pouch are rolled in. Almost 50 species are known from Europe, Asia and North and South America. Many are fully hardy and can be grown outside in temperate gardens; others are more suitable for alpine house or cool greenhouse culture. Until recently, species have been difficult to obtain as all are strictly protected in the wild, but as more nurseries grow them from seed and growers learn how to accommodate their needs, they are becoming more readily available.

Cypripediums do not have tubers or fleshy roots but a thin, rather woody creeping underground stem that rots if kept too wet and shrivels if kept too dry. Most species like a well-drained soil that is not rich in organic matter. Two suggested compost mixes are:

Mix 1

2 parts medium bark
2 parts fine bark
2 parts leaf mould
2 parts perlite
1 part coarse sand

Coelogyne trinerve.

Mix 2

4 parts Seramis
1 part loam (such as John Innes 3)

The following two species are attractive plants for a cool greenhouse.

C. formosanum

has an opposite pair of round, pleated leaves and a white or pale pink flower with darker spots. It flowers in summer.

C. japonicum

grows wild in Japan, Korea and China and is similar to *C. formosanum* but the flowers have pale yellow or yellow-green sepals spotted with purple at the base, and the lip is whitish or yellowish pink, veined and spotted with red. It is rather more temperamental than *C. formosanum*.

Dendrobium loddigesii

Dendrobium

This is one of the largest of all orchid genera with about 1,000 species widespread in Asia and Australasia. These plants have pseudobulbs of all shapes and sizes and grow in climates ranging from hot, humid tropical lowlands to near alpine conditions on mountains. With such a range, it is difficult to generalize, but while some of the small species grow well mounted on bark, most are grown in baskets or pots (as small as possible) in a fairly coarse, free-draining mix.

Many species, particularly those from India and Australia, like warm, sunny conditions in summer but will not flower unless given cool, dry and bright conditions in winter.

D. aphylla
(synonym *D. pierardii*) is a very pretty species with long, slender, cane-like pseudobulbs, leafy when young but the leaves soon fall. Pale pink flowers, with a primrose yellow trumpet-shaped lip, are borne all along the leafless stems in spring.

D. kingianum
is a widespread Australian species and is one of the easiest of all orchids to grow. Usually 20–30cm (8–12in) tall, it quickly forms dense clumps and has pale to deep pink flowers in winter, although many different colour forms are known.

Dendrobium nobile hybrid

If the plant is not properly dried off in winter, it produces keikis on the stems instead of flowers.

D. lindleyi

(synonym *D. aggregatum*) is a small, neat species with rectangular pseudobulbs, short, stiff, oval leaves and pendent clusters of golden yellow flowers.

D. loddigesii

has a creeping habit and is better in a basket or on a raft. When dried off properly in winter, it flowers profusely in spring with lilac flowers with an orange blotch on the lip.

D. nobile

and its hybrids are beautiful plants that are widely grown but they do not flower freely if they are not kept cool and dry in winter. They have clusters of stout canes about 50–75cm (20–30in) tall, with leaves that last for two years. The flowers arise along both leafless and leafy stems. *D. nobile* itself has white or pink flowers about 6cm (2½in) in diameter; the lip has a maroon blotch edged with yellow. The Yamamoto hybrids derived from this species are spectacular plants that come in a wide range of colours.

Disa uniflora

Disa

About 130 species of terrestrial orchids from tropical and South Africa with some in Madagascar, but only one species is widely grown. *Disa uniflora* from the Cape Province of South Africa, and its hybrids, are becoming more popular in cultivation as people learn how to grow them.

Disa uniflora

(synonym *D. grandiflora*) grows up to 60cm (24in) tall, with leaves in a rosette at the base and more scattered up the stem, decreasing in size. There are usually from one to three flowers, but occasionally there are as many as ten (in spite of the name), up to 10cm (4in) in diameter, with one of the sepals forming a shallow hood enclosing the petals and the other sepals. The most common

colour is bright red, but yellow and pink forms are known.

Plants often reproduce by stolons and can form large clumps. Unlike most terrestrial orchids, *D. uniflora* never goes completely dormant and should not be dried off. Plants will not tolerate rich soil and need acid conditions (pH 5–6) and very pure water so it is always safer to use rainwater. Try not to get water on to the leaves.

Some growers use completely inert potting composts such as coarse grit; others use a mixture such as sphagnum moss, fibrous peat and chopped bracken. Perhaps the most successful is sphagnum moss alone. As sphagnum tends to deteriorate over time, it is better to repot annually, either in autumn or early spring.

Disa uniflora can withstand temperatures as low as 5°C (40°F), possibly even lower. Good light is important otherwise plants become rather drawn and spindly and the flower colour is less intense.

Plants grown in completely inorganic composts obviously need to be fed, but fertilizer should not be applied at more than one quarter strength, and only when the plants are actively growing in spring and early summer and in autumn when new tubers are being formed. The original tuber that gave rise to the flowering shoot dies after flowering and at least one new tuber is then formed.

Hybrids

The first hybrid, *Disa* Veitchii, (*D. uniflora* x *D. racemosa*) was registered in 1891, but by 1922 only 11 *Disa* hybrids had been registered. In 1981, *Disa* Kirstenbosch Pride (*D. uniflora* x *D. cardinalis*) was registered and this lovely plant seemed to give a boost to further hybridization. By the end of 1995, 135 hybrids had been registered and the number increases each year. Almost all are based on *D. uniflora* and one or more of a mere six or so other species.

They are beautiful plants but most are rather similar in general appearance with tall spikes of orange-red, orange or pink flowers. All should be cultivated in the same way as *D. uniflora*. Good hybrids include:

Betty's Bay
Diores (different cultivars may be pink, red or orange)
Foam
Frieda Duckitt
Helmut Meyer
Kalahari Sands
Kewensis
Kirstenbosch Pride
Langleyensis
Veitchii

Encyclia

This genus includes about 150 species of orchids from subtropical and tropical America and the West Indies, closely related to *Epidendrum* and at one time included in that genus. Most species have prominent pseudobulbs, usually round or ovoid. The smaller species can be mounted on a bark slab; the larger ones are grown in a shallow pot or a basket in a coarse bark mix. Most species like good light and a dry winter rest.

E. citrina
has grey-green leaves up to 25cm (10in) long and scented, lemon yellow to golden yellow flowers in spring and summer. Although of medium size, this species is better mounted on bark because of its pendulous growth habit.

E. cochleata
is known as the cockleshell orchid because of its shell-shaped lip. Along with some relatives it has recently been transferred to another genus,

Encyclia vitellina

Prosthechea, but it is still usually known as *Encyclia*. The pseudobulbs are large and pear shaped, up to 25cm (10in) long, each with one to three leaves. The flower spike is erect, up to 50cm (20in) tall, with several yellow-green flowers with a deep purple, shell-shaped lip held on top of the flower. The ribbon-like sepals and petals hang down and are about 8cm (3in) long. *E. chacaoensis* is similar to *E. cochleata* with cream or pale green flowers with the lip veined in red.

E. polybulbon

is a dwarf species with small two-leaved pseudobulbs set on a creeping stem. The solitary flowers appear in autumn and winter and are large for such a small plant, with yellow-bronze sepals and petals and a white lip. This species can be mounted or grown in a shallow pan.

E. vitellina

has grey-green leaves and an erect spike of bright orange-red flowers about 3cm (1in) in diameter, in autumn and winter. It is an easy and cheerful plant.

Lemboglossum

There are about 14 species of *Lemboglossum* from Central America and Mexico; they were formerly included in *Odontoglossum*. They have clumps of round or ovoid pseudobulbs. The flowers are showy, of various colours, often barred or spotted. Grow them in shallow pots in a fairly coarse bark mix or mounted on bark.

L. bictoniense

(synonym *Odontoglossum bictoniense*) has an erect, many-flowered spike up to 80cm (32in) tall with scented flowers about 5cm (2in) diameter, usually green-

Lemboglossum rossii

ish marked with brown and a white or pink lip. Various colour forms known.

L. cervantesii

(synonym *Odontoglossum cervantesii*) has spikes up to 30cm (12in) tall with two to eight white or pink flowers with broken bands of brown in the lower half, and a white or pink lip with purple stripes at the base. It flowers in winter.

L. rossii

(synonym *Odontoglossum rossii*) is similar to *O. cervantesii* but the sepals and base of the petals are spotted. It flowers in winter.

Lycaste

This genus contains about 45 species found from Mexico through Central America to Peru and Bolivia. The pseudobulbs are large with big, pleated leaves. The long-lasting, erect flowers arise singly at the base of a pseudobulb and have large, spreading sepals. Grow in a coarse bark mix in a shallow pot in light shade. Water and feed freely while growing and provide good ventilation.

L. aromatica
has cinnamon-scented, bright yellow flowers about 8cm (3in) diameter, in winter or spring.

L. lasioglossa
has large orange-brown flowers with a yellow lip, in winter to spring.

L. skinneri
is the National Flower of Guatemala. The flowers are white or pink with a darker lip, up to 15cm (6in) in diameter and appear in winter or early spring. **Jackpot** is a good hybrid with large yellow flowers with darker dots.

Lycaste clinta

Masdevallia

Masdevallia includes about 350 species of evergreen epiphytic or lithophytic orchids found in Central and South America, often at high altitudes. Their slender stems bear one thick-textured leaf. The sepals are much larger than the petals and lip, and are joined at the base. This results in flowers that are triangular in appearance or more or less tubular, with just the ends of the sepals spreading. The sepals often have long 'tails'. These small plants form dense clumps and often flower off and on throughout the year. They have become very popular with growers as they take up little space and are brightly coloured and free flowering. *Masdevallia* belongs to the Pleurothallid group of orchids.

Most species must have cool conditions and should not be allowed to dry out completely, but are susceptible to rot if overwatered; once this has been mastered, they are easily grown. They are most often grown in a fine bark, usually with perlite and chopped sphagnum mixed in, but can be grown in pure sphagnum moss. Many species can tolerate night-time temperatures as low as 10°C (50°F), but few can withstand temperatures over 26°C (80°F) for more than a short time. They like light shade, high humidity and good air movement. If the humidity can be kept up, they are good windowsill plants.

M. barlaeana
is a medium-sized plant with red, bell-shaped flowers about 4cm (1½in) long.

M. caudata
has scented pink flowers with long yellow tails, mostly in spring.

Masdevallia coccinea

M. coccinea

(synonyms *M. harryana* and *M. lindenii*) is a robust and variable species with flowers held well above the leaves. The colour of the long-lasting flowers ranges from white to yellow, red and magenta.

Late spring and summer species
M. coriacea
(synonym *M. uniflora*) is a medium-sized plant with thick leaves and fleshy, cup-shaped flowers, variable in colour but usually white flushed with purple.
M. daviesii
has bright yellow, long-lasting flowers on relatively long stalks.
M. ignea
has yellow, orange or bright red flowers.
M. prodigiosa
has wide apricot or orange flowers with backward-pointing tails, mostly in spring.
M. veitchiana
is a robust and showy plant; flowers are bright orange with bands of purple hairs. Flowers in spring and summer.

Hybrids
Many *Masdevallia* hybrids were made around the end of the 19th century, then few until relatively recently. The hybrids are often more easily grown than the species and flower freely, often off and on throughout the year.
Angel Frost yellow or orange flowers.
Canary yellow or orange flowers.
Copper Angel yellow or orange flowers.
Diana has white flowers with red stripes and yellow tails.
Kimballiana yellow or orange flowers.
Marimba has long-lasting, long-tailed orange to red flowers with darker spots.
Pelican yellow flowers with dark red spots.
Pink Mist in spite of the name, this has creamy flowers tinged with yellow.

Masdevallia Kimballiana

Maxillaria tenuifolia

Maxillaria

There are over 300 species of *Maxillaria* in subtropical and tropical America but relatively few are in cultivation. They are variable in size, with small to large pseudobulbs, usually each with one leaf. Each spike has just one flower in red, brown, yellow or white, which is rarely showy, but interesting. Most are easily grown and do well in an open bark mix in light shade. Keep drier in winter.

M. coccinea
is a dwarf species with a creeping stem and rose pink to scarlet flowers in summer.

M. cucullata
is a variable but free-flowering species; flowers are yellow to brown or almost black, usually striped and spotted with maroon.

M. grandiflora
is one of the bigger species with large, showy, nodding white flowers, which, in the variety *amesiana*, are flushed with pink.

M. picta
has yellow flowers spotted with purple.

M. ubatubana
is similar but a slightly larger plant with bigger flowers.

M. sanderiana
is possibly the showiest species, similar to *M. grandiflora* but the white flowers are 10–15cm (4–6in) in diameter and are marked with red. It is best grown in a basket as the flowers can grow up, down or sideways. Flowers appear in autumn.

M. tenuifolia
is the most widely grown species. It has coconut-scented flowers, usually dark red marked with yellow but sometimes mostly yellow.

Neofinetia

This genus contains one species from Japan and Korea, related to *Angraecum*. Plants can be mounted, but usually do better potted in a fine bark mix. Do not water until the compost has dried out. It will grow in cool or intermediate temperatures, moderate shade and high humidity.

N. falcata

(synonym *Angraecum falcatum*) is a neat plant up to about 20cm (8in) high, often branched at the base and forming clumps. The flowers are white, about 2.5cm (1in) in diameter, with a slender spur, and appear in summer. This species has been widely grown for a long time in Japan, where there are many selected varieties, including ones with pink flowers such as 'Tamahime', and others with variegated leaves. 'Amami Island' has larger flowers than usual.

Neofinetia falcata

Pleurothallis isthmica

Pleurothallis

A large genus with about 1,000 species found in tropical America. Most are small plants with slender, single-leafed stems and small flowers. Few are showy but they have many enthusiasts. Pot in a fine bark mix or sphagnum; they like high humidity and cool to intermediate temperatures and are very suitable for an orchid case.

P. grobyi

has green, white or yellow-orange flowers, marked with purple or red, in summer.

P. lanceana

has many yellow flowers, tinged with red.

P. schiedii

is a tiny and fascinating species only 2.5–5cm (1–2in) tall. The flowers are light brown and the edges of the sepals are fringed with pendent blobs of white wax.

P. sonderiana

is another tiny plant with lots of long-lasting, small orange flowers.

Promenea xanthina

Promenea

There are about 15 species of these dwarf epiphytes found in Brazil. They have small, clustered pseudobulbs, grey-green leaves and relatively large, fleshy flowers. Pot in a free-draining compost.

P. guttata
is less than 8cm (3in) tall; the flowers are bright yellow barred with red, the lip is dark purple at the base, and the tip yellow.

P. stapelioides
has cream to beige flowers, heavily banded with maroon, with a purple lip, in summer.

P. xanthina
(also known as *P. citrina*) has primrose yellow flowers with a bright yellow lip, in summer.

Rossioglossum

This genus contains six species from Mexico and Central America, closely related to *Odontoglossum*. The flowers are large and showy, usually yellow with brown markings. Grow in a standard compost in a shallow pot or basket. Give plenty of water and fertilizer while in growth but keep drier and cooler in winter.

R. grande
(synonym *Odontoglossum grande*) is called the clown orchid. The flower spikes are about 30cm (12in) long, each with about eight flowers. The flowers are 15cm (6in) in diameter with yellow sepals, barred and dotted with chestnut brown. The petals are yellow with a brown base and the lip is cream or pale yellow, banded with red and brown. The yellow and red callus is supposed to resemble a clown. Flowers appear in autumn and winter.

Rossioglossum grande

Sarcochilus hartmannii

Sarcochilus

This genus comprises about 15 species of dwarf orchids from Australia and South East Asia. They are compact plants that can be mounted on bark or potted in a fairly coarse mix and like light shade and high humidity with good air movement.

S. hartmannii

has stems that branch at the base to form clumps. The waxy white flowers are spotted with maroon in the centre and are up to 3cm (1in) in diameter. They are good plants for a windowsill or orchid case.

Sophronitis

About seven dwarf species from high altitudes in Bolivia, Paraguay and eastern Brazil. The flowers are showy, large for the size of plant, usually red but sometimes bright pink or orange. They like shady, humid conditions and good ventilation and can be grown in small pots in fine bark compost or mounted on a slab. They are slow to establish and should be divided as little as possible; a well-established plant is a spectacular mass of colour when in flower.

Species of *Sophronitis* have been much used in hybridization with relatives such as *Cattleya* and *Laelia* for the small size and bright colours they bring to a cross.

Sophrocattleya Jewel Box 'Darkwaters'

Sophronitis coccinea (synonym *S. grandiflora*)

S. cernua
has orange-red flowers about 3cm (1in) in diameter.
S. coccinea
(synonym *S. grandiflora*) is a free-flowering plant with fleshy flowers 8cm (3in) in diameter, usually bright scarlet with yellow at the base of the lip, but other colour forms exist. The variety *aurantiaca* is orange, *purpurea* is purple and *rossiteriana* is yellow. Flowers are borne in winter.

Stenoglottis

Five or six species of *Stenoglottis* are known from tropical East Africa and South Africa. They are quite small plants with cylindrical, tuberous roots; the leaves form a rosette with the flower spike arising in the centre. All the species look rather similar and all are easily grown, attractive plants that do well in a cool greenhouse or on a windowsill.In the wild, they often grow in a thin layer of moss or soil on top of a rock but do well in a free-draining terrestrial compost or a fine bark mix. After flowering, or sometimes even while the plant is still in flower, the leaves start to die back. Pick off the dead leaves and keep the plant dry until signs of new growth appear, usually after two or three months.*Stenoglottis* plants can be easily propagated by division. Each tuberous root has a growing point at one end, but they look better when allowed to form a good clump.

S. fimbriata
has attractive, wavy-edged leaves, heavily spotted with purple. The late summer flowers are pink with a three-lobed, purple-spotted fringed lip.
S. longifolia
is the tallest species, with a flower spike reaching up to 50cm (20in), and is the most common in cultivation. The leaves are plain green often with wavy edges; the autumn flowers are pink with a purple-spotted, five-lobed lip.
S. woodii
is a small plant; the flower spike grows up to 20cm (8in) tall. The leaves are plain green, the flowers are usually white but there is a pink form. It flowers in summer, earlier than the other species.

The most popular orchids that are suitable for an intermediate greenhouse are cattleyas and laelias and their hybrids, *Miltoniopsis* hybrids (pansy orchids), *Phalaenopsis* (moth orchids) and paphiopedilums (slipper orchids), but many other orchids will also grow happily in these conditions.

Orchids for the intermediate greenhouse
minimum night-time temperature **15°C(60°F)**

8

Orchids for the intermediate greenhouse

Aerangis

African orchids are increasing in popularity and species of *Aerangis* are among the most desirable. There are about 50 species in Africa and Madagascar; most are small or medium in size. The leaves are usually thick-textured, in most species wider near the apex than the base.

They have arching or pendent spikes of elegantly shaped, spurred white flowers sometimes tinged with salmon pink or rusty red, almost all strongly and sweetly scented at night. With a few exceptions, they like shady, humid conditions with good air movement. They do well mounted on bark provided the humidity is high enough, but they will grow in pots in a free-draining compost. Almost all thrive in intermediate conditions, and any species that can be obtained is worth growing.

A. articulata,

from Madagascar, has greyish-green leaves often edged with reddish-purple and long sprays of pure white flowers.

A. brachycarpa

is one of the larger species from tropical Africa. It has dark green, luxuriant leaves and long sprays of white flowers.
A. confusa, from Kenya, is similar but has slightly smaller, more strongly pink-tinged flowers. It is very reliable and sometimes flowers twice a year.

A. citrata

is a small species from Madagascar with long sprays of creamy white, occasionally creamy yellow flowers, very freely borne.

A. distincta,

from Malawi, was only described in

Aerangis luteoalba var. *rhodosticta*

1987 but is already well established in cultivation. The leaves are deeply bilobed at the tip, resembling a fish tail. The flowers are large with pink-tipped sepals and long spurs. There are two forms, one flowering in spring, the other in late summer.

A. fastuosa

is a small species from Madagascar, with dark green leaves, that produces a mass of large, pure white flowers on shorter spikes than most.

A. kotschyana

is a tropical African species with broad, dark green leaves and long sprays of white flowers with a salmon pink spur up to 25cm (10in) long with a corkscrew twist in the middle. Intermediate to warm conditions required with moderate shade; keep drier in winter. This species does better when mounted; if it is potted, the compost should be coarse and free-draining.

A. luteoalba var. rhodosticta

is a small but very distinctive species from East Africa that flowers from an early age. The leaves are narrow and dark green; flowers are creamy white with a red column.

A. mystacidii

is another of the smaller species but is free flowering and reliable. It is a neat plant with dark green leaves and white, pink-tinged flowers with a spur up to 8cm (3in) long.

A. verdickii

is a distinctive species from East Africa with fleshy, grey-green leaves, often with undulating, purple edges. The strongly scented flowers are white with spurs up to 20cm (8in) long. The thick roots and succulent leaves show that this species is adapted to a harsh dry season and it should be kept almost dry when not in active growth. It likes only light shade and is better mounted; again, if potted it should be in a very coarse mix.

Aeranthes caudata

Aeranthes

There are 30–40 species of *Aeranthes* in Madagascar and the other Indian Ocean islands, with two species in Zimbabwe. They appeal to people who like strange flowers; they are not conventionally showy but always attract attention when in flower. They have short stems and leaves forming a fan. The flowers are green, yellow-green or greenish-white and are usually borne dangling on long, wiry, pendent spikes. Most have fine roots and grow better in a pot in a fairly fine compost. Hang up when the plant is in flower. They prefer humid, shady conditions.

A. grandiflora

has bright green leaves and yellow-green or greenish-white flowers. *A. arachnites* is similar but slightly smaller.

A. henricii

looks very different from all other *Aeranthes* species. The leaves are dark green, the roots thick and often flattened. The flowers are green and white, almost 20cm (8in) in diameter, with a slender spur 15cm (6in) long. It is a striking plant but can be reluctant to flower.

Aerangis mystacidii

Angraecum didieri

Angraecum

There are about 200 species of *Angraecum* in Africa and Madagascar, which range in size from very small to very large. They have white, green or yellow-green flowers with a long or short spur. Species with white, long-spurred flowers are pollinated by night-flying moths and are strongly scented in the evening and at night. Most species grow well in pots in a medium or coarse bark mix, depending on size.

A. calceolus
is a compact, medium-sized plant with branched spikes of yellow-green flowers. It is not showy but is easily grown and rarely out of flower.

A. compactum
is a neat plant with dark green leaves and large, pure white flowers. It likes a humid, shady situation.

A. didieri
is one of the best species for anyone who is short of space. The plants are small with narrow, dark green leaves and warty roots. The flowers are large for the size of plant, and are pure white with long spurs. It likes moderate shade and grows well mounted provided the

humidity is high; otherwise pot in medium bark. *A. rutenbergianum* is similar but has slightly smaller flowers.

A. germinyanum
is a variable species with long, slender stems and white flowers with a shell-shaped lip held uppermost; the sepals and petals are long and spidery; the spur is long and slender. It grows well potted or mounted in shady, humid conditions.

A. leonis
has a short stem with a fan of fleshy, flattened leaves. The flowers are large and white with a funnel-shaped lip at the base and a long spur.

A. magdalenae
is one of the finest species. It is a medium-sized plant with dark green leaves forming a fan and large, pure white flowers with a strong, spicy scent in the evening. In the wild it grows on rocks in only light shade, and so it prefers good light. Pot in a coarse mix and keep drier in winter.

A. sesquipedale,
the comet orchid, is one of the best known species. The medium to large plants have large, waxy, creamy-white flowers with a spur up to 30cm (12in) long, in winter. It thrives in warmer parts of an intermediate house, in good light.

Angraecum sesquipedale

Anguloa

About ten species of *Anguloa* occur in the South American Andes. They are large plants, related to *Lycaste*, with big pseudobulbs and pleated leaves which last for only one season. The flowers are cup-shaped, usually yellow, and sometimes marked with red-brown. Flowers are produced singly at the base of a pseudobulb. Plants require ample feeding and water while in growth but should be kept almost dry while dormant. They should be grown in the cooler parts of an intermediate house.

Anguloa clowesii

A. clowesii
has scented lemon or golden yellow flowers.
A. uniflora
has creamy white flowers flushed with pink and with red spots near the base.

Angulocaste
(Anguloa x Lycaste)

These are large plants with very big, pleated leaves. They have one or two tulip-shaped flowers on long stems arising from the base of plant. They require shady, intermediate conditions; keep them dry in winter.
Andromeda large pink flowers spotted with red.
Apollo 'Goldcourt' greenish-yellow flowers with red spots.
Aurora red and orange flowers.
Gemini mahogany-red sepals and creamy yellow petals dotted with red.
Wyld Charm deep pink flowers.
Wyld Delight scented yellow flowers with red dots.

Angulocaste Apollo

Ascocenda Princess Mikasa

Ascocenda
(*Ascocentrum* x *Vanda*)

These hybrids have become very popular as they require less light to flower, tolerate lower temperatures and are smaller plants than vandas, but have larger flowers than ascocentrums. The flowers are brightly coloured and long lasting. Here are a few of the named hybrids available:

Bangkok freely produced orange-peach flowers with an orange-red lip.
Dong Tarn bright red flowers with maroon spots.
Madame Nok yellow flowers with dark red spots; the mid lobe of the lip is red.
Meda Arnold deep pink or red flowers.
Pak-Chong lime green flowers with a white column.
Princess Mikasa 'Blue Velvet' deep violet blue flowers.
Suk Samran Beauty 'Surat Pink', AM/RHT large pink flowers.
Sunkist yellow flowers.
Tan Chai Beng 'Violet Delight' violet flowers.

Tubtim Velvet white flowers, tipped with pink.
Udomchai orange flowers.
Yip Sum Wah smallish but vivid orange flowers.

Brassavola

This genus includes about 15 species of orchid in tropical America, related to *Cattleya*. They have small pseudobulbs with one fleshy leaf at the apex and medium-sized or large green and white flowers, scented in the evening. They prefer good light and can be mounted or grown in pots or baskets. They like cool to intermediate night-time temperatures, but do not mind high daytime temperatures. Species of *Brassavola* have been used a lot in hybridization with *Cattleya* and other relatives.

B. cucullata
has pendent leaves up to 25cm (10in) long and large, greenish-white flowers in autumn with long, drooping sepals and

petals. The lip has a long, slender tip.
B. digbyana
See *Rhyncholaelia digbyana*.
B. nodosa
(synonym *B. venosa*) This attractive species has large, greenish-white or cream flowers with a white lip, strongly scented in the evening. Flowers are borne in winter.
B. tuberculata
(synonyms *B. fragrans* and *B. perrinii*) This plant has long leaves that are almost cylindrical, but grooved on top. The summer flowers are creamy yellow or lime-green, sometimes with red spots, and a white lip, sometimes with green or yellow in the throat.

Brassia

This genus includes about 25 species of epiphytic orchid from tropical America. The ovoid pseudobulbs each have one or two leaves and the plants bear large, spidery, showy flowers with long, narrow sepals and petals. Grow them in coarse bark in a pot or basket; feed and water freely in summer but keep almost dry in winter.

B. caudata
has arched flower spikes up to 80cm (32in) long with the flowers in two rows. The summer flowers are yellow or orange, usually marked with red-brown; the lip is yellow or green. The lateral sepals have long, slender tails up to 18cm (7in) long.

Brassia verrucosa

B. maculata
has yellow-green flowers with purple marks in early summer.

B. verrucosa
has pale yellow to lime green flowers with brown spots. The white lip has red spots at the base and prominent green warts; the sepals are up to 12cm (5in) long. Flowers appear in spring and early summer.

B. Rex
(B. verrucosa x gireoudiana)
has spidery flowers larger than those of either parent, in pale green with brown spots and green warts. Many cultivars have received awards, including 'Barbara', AM/AOS and 'Tacoma', AM/AOS.

Bulbophyllum

With over 1,000 species found throughout the tropics, this is one of the largest orchid genera. Plants have a creeping, woody stem with large or small pseudobulbs set either close together or well spaced out, each with one or two thick-textured leaves. The flowers vary from showy to small and dull-coloured, but many are bizarrely shaped and often attract attention. Species in the section *Cirrhopetalum* (originally a genus in its own right and still considered as such by some authorities) have large flowers coming off at almost the same height at the top of the flowering stem.

Species where the pseudobulbs form clumps do well potted in a fine but well-drained bark mix, but when the pseudobulbs are set far apart, plants keep climbing out of a pot and are better in a basket or on a slab of bark. In the wild they occur at a wide range of altitudes but in cultivation most will grow

Bulbophyllum graveolens

in intermediate temperatures. Most like good light and should be kept fairly dry when not actively growing; they should be watered with care while new growth is developing as that tends to rot with too much moisture.

B. barbigerum
is a small West African species with round, flat, pale green, single-leafed pseudobulbs and deep maroon-purple flowers in summer. The lip is fringed with long hairs clubbed at the tips. It does better mounted.

B. lobbii
is a striking species from South East Asia. The large summer flowers are usually yellow, streaked and spotted with red-brown.

B. longiflorum
(synonym *Cirrhopetalum umbellatum*) is a widespread species found from Africa through Asia to Australia. The flowers are about 3cm (1in) long, usually mottled light and dark purple, but sometimes they are bronze or clear yellow.

B. macranthum
is a large-flowered species from Burma with yellowish or speckled purple flowers about 5cm (2in) in diameter in early summer.

B. medusae

(synonym *Cirrhopetalum medusae*) is a species from South East Asia with round heads of spidery cream flowers with a strange, tangled appearance, in winter.

B. rothschildianum

(synonym *Cirrhopetalum rothschildianum*), from India, has striking but unpleasant-smelling, maroon flowers mottled with yellow, in winter.

B. sandersonii

is an African species in which part of the flower spike is swollen but flattened, and often purple. The deep purple, occasionally yellow, flowers are arranged along either side. It is a strange-looking plant that always causes comment when it is in flower. *B. scaberulum* and *B. purpureorhachis* are similar in general appearance.

Hybrids

Several hybrids exist, most involving species in section *Cirrhopetalum*, but only one seems to be readily available.

Bulbophyllum Elizabeth Ann (B. longissimum x B. rothschildianum)

has pendent sprays of pink-mauve flowers. The cultivar 'Bucklebury' is outstanding and has received an AM from both the RHS and the AOS.

Calanthe

This genus includes about 150 species of medium to large terrestrial orchids found in tropical and subtropical Africa, Asia and Australia, with most species in Asia. The pseudobulbs are small to large; the evergreen or deciduous leaves are pleated. Plants need a free-draining terrestrial compost and a shady position; they do better if repotted every year in spring. The deciduous species grow at intermediate temperatures but the evergreen species are more suited to an alpine house. They seem to have been more widely grown in the past than they are now.

Deciduous species

These should be kept dry in a cool, bright place after the leaves are shed, or they will not flower. The flowers appear in late winter, before the leaves.

C. rosea

has pink flowers with a darker lip.

C. vestita

is widespread in South East Asia. The flowers are creamy white with a yellow blotch on the lip but there are many

Calanthe St. Brelade

colour forms, including the variety *rubro-maculata* with a red-purple blotch on the lip and *williamsii*, which is pale pink with a crimson lip.

Hybrids
Many attractive hybrids are available and most are rather large plants.
Diana Broughton deep rose pink.
Sedenii white.
Veitchii pale pink.
William Murray white with a red-purple blotch on the lip.

Cattleya

Cattleyas are the stereotypical orchids and used to be very popular as corsages. There are about 50 species in tropical Central and South America. Most have large pseudobulbs with one or two leaves each, set on a stout, creeping stem. The flowers are large and showy, with spreading sepals and petals and a lip that is often trumpet-shaped with frilly edges. They are usually grown in wide, shallow pots or baskets in a coarse bark mix and like good light. They need plenty of water and fertilizer while in growth and a drier, cooler rest in winter. The leaves enclose a sheath from which flowers appear. Cattleyas are divided into unifoliate (single-leafed) and bifoliate (two-leaved) species.

Unifoliate species
C. labiata
was the first of the large-flowered species to be brought into cultivation. The flowers are as large as 15cm (6in) in diameter, typically pale to deep pink with a magenta lip with a yellow blotch at the base, but there are many named and awarded varieties. All flower in autumn.

Cattleya labiata

C. eldorado, *C. gaskelliana*, *C. perce-valiana*, *C. warneri* and *C. warscewiczii* are all rather similar and are often confused with *C. labiata*.
C. maxima
is a species from Ecuador, Colombia and Peru with large, lilac-pink flowers. The lip has purple veins and a yellow mark in the throat. It flowers in winter.

Bifoliate species
These species need a slightly longer winter rest. They tend to be smaller plants than the unifoliate species.
C. amethystoglossa
has up to 20 flowers on the spike, each about 10cm (4in) in diameter. The sepals and petals are white or pale pink with purple spots; the lip is magenta. Flowers appear in spring.
C. aurantiaca
is a free-flowering Central American species with relatively small, bright orange flowers in summer.
C. bicolor
is an elegant species from Brazil with flowers up to 9cm (3½in) in diameter. The sepals and petals are greenish-bronze, the lip is magenta-purple. Late summer to autumn flowers.

Cattleya trianaei

C. intermedia
has large, strongly scented flowers with lilac or white sepals and petals and a purple, lilac or white lip in summer.

C. skinneri
is the National Flower of Costa Rica. It has rose pink or purple flowers in early summer and is a good windowsill plant.

Hybrids
These are so numerous it is possible to mention only a very few.

Angel Bells white flowers.

Bob Betts 'White Wings' large, well-shaped white flowers in spring.

Bow Bells white flowers with a yellow blotch in the throat in autumn.

Chocolate Drop many smallish, orange-red flowers.

Dale Edward salmon pink flowers.

Guatemalensis smallish, salmon pink flowers in spring. A natural hybrid.

Lamartine white flowers with a gold lip, edged with pink.

Portia 'Coerulea' lavender blue flowers in autumn.

Intergeneric hybrids
All *Cattleya* species are beautiful but many make large, sprawling plants. They have been extensively crossed with related genera, such as *Brassavola*, *Epidendrum*, *Laelia* and *Sophronitis*, and many of the hybrids, particularly more recent ones, produce large flowers on compact plants, sometimes called mini-cattleyas or mini-cats. Hybrids involving *Sophronitis* tend to be compact plants with relatively large, brightly coloured flowers.

Brassocattleya
(Brassavola x Cattleya)
Fuchs Star starry white flowers with a broad lip veined with mauve.

Pluto large, strongly scented pale green flowers with a fringed lip.

Touraine white flowers; the lip is large and edged with mauve.

Brassolaeliocattleya
(Brassavola x Cattleya x Laelia)
Fortune yellow with a red lip.

Good as Gold bright yellow.

Jungle Treasure miniature plant; yellow flowers with a red lip.

Cattleya aurantiaca

Potinaria Sunrise

Pumpkin Festival bright red flowers.
Yellow Imp 'Golden Grail', AM/AOS –
bright yellow.

Laeliocattleya
(Cattleya x Laelia)

These plants come in a range of colours.
Angel Heart 'Hihimauu' Pink and
white scented flowers, marked with
darker pink.
Barbara Belle 'Apricot' apricot
yellow flowers.
Beaumesnil 'Parme' bright magenta
flowers with a yellow lip and purple
stripes.
Daniris large yellow flowers with a
purple and gold lip.
El Corrito yellow flowers.
Georges Issaly large, mauve flowers.
Irene Finney mauve flowers with a
darker lip.
Schilleriana
a natural hybrid between *Laelia purpu-
rata* and *Cattleya intermedia*; usually
white with a purple lip but there are
other colour forms.
Stradivarius 'Eclipse' salmon pink
with a yellow lip.

Tropical Pointer 'Cheetah' orange
with brown spots.

Potinara
(Brassavola x Cattleya x Laelia x
Sophronitis)

Haw Yuan Gold 'D-J' rich golden
yellow flowers.
Sunrise light magenta flowers with a
darker lip, orange at the base.

Sophrocattleya
(Cattleya x Sophronitis)

Angel Face miniature; bright pink
flowers with a pink-fringed yellow lip.
Crystelle Smith 'Nathan's Reward',
HCC/AOS bright pink flowers with a
yellow lip.

Sophrolaeliocattleya
(Cattleya x Laelia x Sophronitis)

Coastal Sunrise has several cultivars
including 'Lemon Chiffon' (yellow), 'Pink
Surprise' (pinkish-purple) and 'Tropico',
HCC/AOS (orange, tinged with purple).
Epsom miniature; pink flowers with a
darker lip.
Ginny Champion 'Prince' miniature;
orange-red flowers, yellow in the centre
with a red lip.
Hazel Boyd 'Royal Scarlet' semi-
miniature plant; bright red and orange,
free-flowering.
Jewel Box 'Sheherezade' carmine red
flowers with a darker lip.
Jungle Bean bright yellow flowers with
a red lip.
Roblar 'Orange Gem' small, bright
orange flowers.
Sutter Creek 'Gold Country',
HCC/AOS – miniature plant with bright
yellow flowers with red-fringed lips.
Tiny Titan miniature; flowers may be
yellow, orange or red, with a red lip.

Dendrochilum javierense

Cyrtorchis praetermissa

Cyrtorchis

Cyrtorchis contains about 15 species of monopodial, epiphytic orchids from tropical Africa and South Africa with waxy, white, scented flowers, with long spurs. Most have thick roots and glossy, bright green leaves. Grow mounted or in pots or baskets in a coarse bark mix, in moderate shade at intermediate temperatures.

C. arcuata

is a widespread species with a woody stem and creamy white flowers 5cm (2in) in diameter. Subspecies *whytei* has broader leaves, larger flowers and a longer spur, up to 10cm (4in) long.

C. chailluana

is the largest species with spidery flowers up to 7.5cm (3in) in diameter and a slender spur to 15cm (6in) long.

C. praetermissa

is a small species with dark green, folded leaves; the spikes have two rows of creamy white flowers with a lily-of-the-valley scent.

Dendrochilum

This genus contains about 120 species of epiphytic orchid from South East Asia, sometimes known as necklace orchids or golden chain orchids. The pseudo-bulbs often form clumps and are of various shapes with one or two leaves each. The flower spikes are graceful, erect at first then arching, with many small flowers. Many species are worth growing but only a few appear in cultivation. They do well in shallow pots with a medium, free-draining compost and are better with a short winter rest. Those with very long spikes need to be suspended when in flower.

D. cobbianum

has conical, single-leafed pseudobulbs and long spikes of white flowers with a yellow lip in autumn.

D. filiforme

has small, clustered pseudobulbs each with two narrow leaves. The slender spike has many scented, yellow flowers in summer.

D. glumaceum

has larger flowers than most. They are white, scented, have large, cream bracts and appear in spring. *D. latifolium* is similar but more vigorous and with smaller bracts.

Epidendrum

There are about 500 species of *Epidendrum* in tropical America. The plants are very variable in size and manner of growth. Some are small, creeping plants while others have tall, reed-like stems. Most species with distinct pseudobulbs are now included in *Encyclia*. Most are epiphytic but a few are terrestrial and some grow on rocks. Apart from small species that are better mounted, they grow well in pots in a bark mix and in an intermediate greenhouse.

E. cinnabarinum

has cane-like stems up to 1m (3ft) tall with many bright orange-red flowers up to 6cm (2½in) across.

E. ibaguense

(synonym *E. radicans*) is a tall plant with cane-like, leafy stems 1–1.5m (3–5ft) high and red flowers with a fringed lip. *E.* O'brienianum is an early hybrid of this species which is widely grown; it is similar with rose red flowers. These plants are easily grown in cool or intermediate

Epidendrum parkinsonianum

conditions, in good light, and flower almost all year round. They are often grown in tropical gardens.

E. parkinsonianum

has narrow, fleshy, pendent leaves 30–50cm (12–20in) long. The flowers are large, scented and long lasting, with yellow-green sepals and petals and a pure white lip. Because of the pendent leaves, it needs to be mounted on bark or in a suspended pot in a coarse bark mix. It prefers fairly good light.

E. porpax

is a small, creeping plant with fleshy yellow-green flowers with a purple lip.

E. pseudepidendrum

is a tall species with lime green sepals and petals and a glossy, bright orange lip. It flowers in winter.

Eulophia

Over 200 species of terrestrial orchids found throughout the tropics and subtropics, with most in tropical and South Africa. Some have chains of underground corms while others have pseudobulbs partly above ground, usually forming clumps; the latter tend to be easier to grow. There are many beautiful species, but unfortunately only a few are available in cultivation. All species have fleshy roots that rot easily, so they need a free-draining compost which should be allowed to dry out before watering again. Plants should be kept dry in winter until signs of new growth are seen in

Eulophia guineensis

spring, when careful watering can start again. As with all terrestrial orchids, it is vitally important to follow the plant's own rhythm. All seem to do well in intermediate conditions in fairly good light.

E. euglossa

has conical, glossy green pseudobulbs up to 20cm (8in) long. The flower spike grows up to 1m (3ft) tall, and bears many green flowers with a white lip veined with pink. Flowers appear in summer. This is a forest plant and appreciates slightly more shade than other species.

E. guineensis

(synonym *E. quartiniana*) has small pseudobulbs and broad, pleated leaves. The flower spike is 30–50cm (12–20in) tall, the flowers are about 5cm (2in) in diameter with narrow, erect, green or purple-brown sepals and petals and a large pink lip with a purple blotch at the base. Flowers are borne in summer.

E. streptopetala

(synonym *E. paiveana*) has ovoid, ribbed pseudobulbs up to 10cm (4in) tall and pleated leaves up to 60cm (24in) long. The spike is 1–1.5m (3–5ft) tall, with many yellow and purple-brown flowers in summer.

Habenaria

This genus contains over 500 species of terrestrial orchids, with tubers or fleshy roots, found throughout the tropics and subtropics, with a few temperate species. Most occur in tropical Africa but only a few are in cultivation. They need a freely drained, open compost and must be kept almost dry while dormant, although a sprinkling of water every few weeks helps to keep tubers from shrivelling. Young shoots are susceptible to rot, so care is needed in watering when growth starts in spring. All seem to be happy in intermediate conditions, in light to moderate shade.

H. procera

is a West African species that is unusual in the genus in that it is usually epiphytic in the wild. The roots are fleshy and some may break off during repotting. These can be used for propagation as they have a growing point at one end. It has a leafy stem and many long-spurred, green and white flowers in summer. Grow in a fine bark mix.

H. rhodocheila

is a striking species from China, Indochina and Malaysia. The spike bears up to 15 flowers; the sepals and petals are green but the three-lobed lip, the largest part of the flower, is yellow, orange or bright red and up to 3cm (1in) long.

Habenaria procera

Habenaria rhodocheila

Laeliocattleya Eva

Jumellea

There are over 50 species of *Jumellea* in Madagascar and the other Indian Ocean islands, with two species on mainland Africa. The stem can be long or short, often branched at the base so that the plants form large clumps, with the leaves usually in two rows. The flowers have long spurs, are white, turning apricot as they age, and are scented in the evening. Although the flowers are borne singly, the effect of a plant scattered with starry, white flowers is beautiful. Grow in intermediate conditions, in moderate shade with high humidity, potted in a medium bark mix.

J. filicornoides
is one of the two African species. The stem can grow up to 30cm (12in) long but is often less, with two rows of dark green leaves and violet-scented white flowers.

J. fragrans
is a species that forms good clumps. The vanilla-scented leaves are used to make a herbal tea.

J. sagittata
has a short stem with several bright, glossy green leaves forming a fan. The flowers are strongly scented after dark, about 8cm (3in) in diameter, with a long spur.

Laelia

There are about 70 species of *Laelia* in Central and South America. They are very closely related to *Cattleya* and many crosses have been made between the two genera. *Laelia* species have single-leafed or two-leaved pseudobulbs, varying in shape from almost globose to cylindrical or club-shaped. The flowers are showy, in many colours – white, pink, mauve, purple, red, orange and yellow - with spreading sepals and petals and a three-lobed lip. The side lobes are often

Jumellea sagittata

Laelia harpophylla

folded over the column so that the lip is trumpet shaped. Most species like intermediate temperatures and good light, with plenty of water and feeding in the growing season, but they need a cool, dry, bright rest in winter to encourage flowering. Many of the Brazilian species are dwarf plants that grow on rocks (often called rupicolous laelias) and a dry winter rest is important for them. They should be given only enough water to prevent the pseudobulbs shrivelling.

L. anceps
has a tall spike with scented white, pink or magenta flowers in winter.

L. autumnalis
has scented, rose-purple flowers with white or yellow on the lip, in autumn. *L. gouldiana* is very similar but flowers in summer.

L. crispa
has white flowers with a purple lip in autumn. *L. lobata* is similar.

L. flava
is a rock-growing species from Brazil with small, ovoid pseudobulbs and clusters of bright yellow flowers in spring or early summer.

L. harpophylla
has tall, slender pseudobulbs and clusters of bright orange flowers in spring. *L. cinnabarina* is similar but less slender with a taller spike of red flowers in spring to early summer.

L. pumila
is a dwarf plant with large, rose-purple flowers in spring or autumn. The lip has a frilly edge, with deep purple and yellow in the throat. It needs more shade than other species.

L. purpurata
is the National Flower of Brazil. It has large and showy flowers, 15–20cm (6–8in) in diameter, usually white or pale pink with a purple lip, but many other colour forms exist. The flowers appear in spring to summer. *L. tenebrosa* is similar but the flowers have copper-bronze sepals and petals and a purple lip.

L. sincorana
is a dwarf, rock-growing species from Brazil with showy, purple flowers.

L. speciosa,
from Mexico, is another dwarf plant with lilac-rose flowers in spring.

Ludisia

Ludisia contains one species of terrestrial orchid from China and South East Asia. This is the most common and easily grown of the jewel orchids, grown for the beauty of their leaves rather than their flowers.

L. discolor
(synonym *Haemaria discolor*) The stem is fleshy, either creeping or erect, and roots at the nodes. The leaves are evergreen, ovate and dark red-brown with red veins, although other colour forms are known. The white or yellow flowers

borne on spikes up to 30cm (12in) tall. This species grows easily in a shallow pan at intermediate or warm temperatures, in shade and with high humidity; it is a good houseplant. It can be grown in a standard houseplant compost with fine bark and perlite mixed in to give free drainage.

Miltoniopsis

These are the pansy orchids. There are five species in Central and South America with large and showy, flat-faced flowers in pink, white or pale yellow. Grow them in a fine bark compost in shade with high humidity.

M. phalaenopsis
is a white-flowered Colombian species with the lip blotched and streaked with red and purple. Flowers are borne in late spring.

Miltoniopsis Beall's Strawberry Joy

M. vexillaria
has white or pale pink flowers in spring. The lip is yellow at the base and streaked with deep pink.

Hybrids
Pansy orchids are popular with growers for their large, long-lasting, scented flowers. The numerous hybrids are have larger flowers than the species and plants tend to be more vigorous. They do well as houseplants provided the humidity can be kept high; if they are too dry, the new leaves, when they appear, are folded in a zigzag.
Alexandre Dumas yellow flowers with red centres.
Anjou mainly deep red with white on the lip; there are several awarded clones including 'St. Patrick', AM/AOS.
Beall's Strawberry Joy pink flowers with a red and white mask.
Celle 'Wasserfal' deep purple-red flowers, the lip streaked and spotted with white giving a waterfall effect.
Emotion the various clones have white, pink or lavender flowers.
Hamburg 'Dark Tower' deep red flowers, some yellow on the lip.
Jean Carlson deep pink flowers with an orange and yellow mask.

Miltoniopsis Robert Strauss

Red Tide large red flowers.
Santa Barbara 'Rainbow Swirl'
white flowers flushed with pink.
St. Helier pink flowers with a white
edge; maroon-red mask.
Zorro 'Yellow Delight' primrose
yellow flowers with a dark mask.

Mystacidium

This genus contains seven to ten
species of small epiphytes from South
Africa and eastern tropical Africa,
rather like small species of *Aerangis*
with spurred white or greenish-yellow
flowers. All species thrive much better
mounted on bark than in a pot.

M. capense,
native to South Africa and Swaziland, is
the most widely grown species. It is a
pretty and free-flowering plant with dark
green leaves and several pendent spikes
each with up to 14 starry white flowers

Mystacidium capense

arranged in 2 rows. It needs good light
and a dryish rest in winter to stimulate
flowering, which should occur in late
spring or early summer.

M. venosum
is similar to *M. capense* but usually
slightly smaller. It flowers in autumn
and early winter and likes light to
moderate shade.

Oncidium

This large genus contains about 500
species in tropical and subtropical
America and is closely related to
Odontoglossum. They vary from very
small to very large plants, with large
or small pseudobulbs and flowers, often
on tall, branched sprays. Many are
brightly coloured, usually yellow, with a
prominent and often lobed lip. Most like
good light and grow at intermediate temperatures. They are usually potted in a
standard compost but very small species
tend to do better mounted on bark.

O. cheirophorum
is a small species from Central America
and Colombia with long, branching
sprays of many scented, yellow flowers
about 2.5cm (1in) in diameter, in summer.

O. cavendishianum
has small pseudobulbs each with one
thick leaf usually described as being
shaped like a mule's ear. The flowers
are bright yellow, spotted with red-
brown. *O. carthagense* is similar, with
cream flowers spotted with magenta.
Flowers are borne in summer.

O. crispum
has large flower sprays in summer, erect
at first but bending over with the weight
of the brown and gold flowers, which
have wavy-edged petals

Oncidium Bois 'Sonja'.

O. maculatum

has many scented, pale yellow flowers with brown spots; the lip has a red crest.

O. pulchellum

See *Tolumnia pulchella*.

O. tigrinum

is a Mexican species with large, flat pseudobulbs and an unbranched spike growing to 40cm (16in) long. The yellow winter flowers have red-brown

Oncidium cheirophorum

bars on the sepals and petals.

O. variegatum

See *Tolumnia variegata*, page 110.

Sharry Baby a famous hybrid with red flowers with white on the lip. 'Sweet Fragrance' is chocolate-scented.

Oncidioda
(Cochlioda x Oncidium)

These hybrids have multicoloured flowers with narrow sepals and petals.
Charlesworthii Branched spikes with many small red flowers with a pink and yellow lip.

Ornithophora

This genus contains two species of dwarf epiphyte from Brazil with pseudobulbs set well apart on the stem. Because of this spreading habit, they are better in a small basket than in a pot; they like good light and plenty of air movement.

O. radicans

(synonym *Sigmatostalix radicans*) An attractive and reliable little plant with lots of small white flowers with a maroon column and yellow anther cap, in late summer.

Paphiopedilum

Slipper orchids have always fascinated growers and their popularity is steadily increasing, not least because of some spectacular new discoveries in recent years. About 70 species are known from South East Asia, from India to the Pacific Islands; most are terrestrial but some are epiphytic or grow on rocks. Although they are sympodial orchids, they do not have pseudobulbs. The leaves are plain green or mottled,

Paphiopedilum Kitty

the latter often purple below.

In most species the flowers are borne singly but in some, there are several flowers on a spike; in that case, the flowers may open all at once or in succession. All have large flowers with the characteristic pouched lip. The petals are spreading or pendulous, sometimes twisted or with hairy warts along the edges.

All paphiopedilums need a free-draining compost – more die from a soggy medium than from any other cause. But as they have no storage organs, they should not remain dry for any length of time and benefit from being repotted every year. A great variety of composts can be used; all growers seem to have their own favourites. Many find rockwool successful, in particular a mix of absorbent rockwool and horticultural foam or coarse perlite. Another widely used mix is three parts of medium bark, one part of peat or peat substitute, one part of coarse perlite, with about half a teaspoon of dolomitic limestone added. Others include a mixture of equal parts of medium and fine bark with ten per cent perlite; and a mixture of medium and fine bark with chopped sphagnum moss.

Humidity should be high and ventilation good. Almost all species grow in an intermediate greenhouse and many do well as windowsill plants or under lights. They like moderate shade although the species with plain green leaves prefer brighter light and slightly more warmth than those with mottled leaves.

P. armeniacum
is a striking Chinese species with mottled leaves and bright golden yellow flowers in spring.

P. barbatum
has mottled leaves and mainly deep purple flowers with white, purple and green stripes in winter and spring. *P. callosum* is similar but with blue-green leaves and larger, lighter flowers with downswept petals, in early summer.

P. delenatii
has attractive, mottled leaves and pale pink flowers with a deeper pink lip in spring. It comes from Vietnam and is one of the few slipper orchids that grow on acidic soils in the wild.

Paphiopedilum Magic Lantern

P. insigne

has plain green leaves and brownish-yellow winter flowers with green and white markings. The variety *sanderae* is green-gold with a white-edged, unspotted dorsal sepal. *P. gratrixianum* is rather similar but the leaves are longer and purple-spotted at the base; the flowers are slightly smaller with fewer dark spots on the dorsal sepal.

P. malipoense

has mottled leaves and a tall flower spike, to 30cm (12in) in height, with unusual raspberry-scented, green flowers veined with purple, in spring. It is a Chinese species, first discovered in 1984.

P. rothschildianum

is one of the finest species with a tall spike of two to five flowers, all open at once, in early summer. The sepals and petals are green-white with purple stripes, the pouch purplish; the petals have a horizontal spread of up to 30cm (12in). In the wild, it is known only from Mount Kinabalu in Borneo, but it is well established in cultivation.

P. victoria-reginae

(also known as *P. chamberlainianum*) is another multi-flowered species, from Sumatra, but the flowers open in succession and not all together. The sepals and twisted petals are green or white, streaked and blotched with purple. The pouch is purple-pink. *P. primulinum*, another Sumatran species, is similar but with slightly smaller, pale yellow flowers.

Hybrids

Over 400 hybrids were known by 1900; now over 10,000 are registered, more than in any other genus. The earliest known hybrid was Harrisianum which first flowered in 1869. *P.* Maudiae (*P. callosum* x *P. lawrenceanum*) was an early and influential hybrid with a green and white flower. 'Magnificum' and 'The Queen' are good cultivars. The breeding of hybrids has the aim of producing single, large flowers that are almost circular in shape with clear colours. White-flowered hybrids include Astarte, F.C. Puddle, Knight's Chalice, Miller's Daughter, Psyche, Shadowfax, White Knight and White Queen. Reds include Dragon Blood and Vintner's Treasure. Royale 'Downland', AM/RHS, has rose pink flowers shaded with green. Winston Churchill has mahogany red and white flowers spotted with red.

Novelty hybrids

These involve a much wider range of species. They are often multi-flowered and need not be circular in shape.

Paphiopedilum Helios

Paphiopedilum Lebaudyanum

Paphiopedilum Lynleigh Koopowitz

Kevin Porter deep pink to red flowers, often with darker chequering.
Lake Shinsei deep yellow flowers.
Lynleigh Koopowitz mainly pink flowers with a mulberry scent.
Magic Lantern pink flowers.
Pearl produces many white flowers together.
Wood Dove large, red-brown flowers.
Yellow Tiger mainly yellow flowers with striped sepals and long petals.

P. rothschildianum hybrids

Some of the best hybrids have involved *P. rothschildianum;* they include:
Delrosi a succession of pink flowers.
St. Swithin white flowers, striped brown with narrow, drooping petals.
Transvaal green and white sepals and spotted and twisted petals; the pouch is pink and yellow.
Vanguard rather similar to Transvaal.

Phalaenopsis

The moth orchids include about 50 species of monopodial epiphytic orchids from Asia and Australasia with short stems and thick, usually somewhat flat-tened, roots. The leaves are plain green or mottled, sometimes large. The flower spike is simple or branched with showy, flat flowers. The lip of the flower has two horn-like projections at the apex.

Grow *Phalaenopsis* in pots or bas-kets in a coarse bark mix, in moderate to heavy shade with high humidity, at inter-mediate to warm temperatures. Water should not be allowed to lodge in the

Paphiopedilum Silberhorn

centre of the plant overnight as this causes rot. Do not be in a hurry to cut off old flower stalks; while they remain green they may branch and flower again. Sometimes keikis are produced on the spike instead of flowers; these can be removed and potted up once they have grown roots. The moth orchids are currently among the most popular of all orchids, widely sold as houseplants. The flowers are long-lasting and they adapt well to windowsill culture, as long as they do not get direct sun. An almost limitless range of hybrids is available, with white, pink or yellow flowers, often striped with another colour.

P. amabilis
(synonym *P. grandiflora*) has glossy, dark green leaves and scented, white, often pink-tinged flowers, the lip with red and yellow marks. This winter-flowering species is in the ancestry of most modern hybrids.

P. equestris
has dark green leaves, often purple below, and arching sprays of many pink flowers around 4cm (1½in) in diameter.

P. mannii
is compact, with dark green leaves and yellow flowers barred with brown.

P. schilleriana,
from the Philippines, has lovely dark green leaves mottled with silver, and branched, many-flowered sprays of white, pink, mauve or purple flowers, mostly in winter. *P. stuartiana*, another Philippine species, has similar leaves and white flowers with the sepals spotted with red-brown at the base.

Hybrids
These are attractive to commercial growers as they can reach flowering size in less than three years from seed. Many are propagated by tissue culture. New hybrids are constantly being registered. They tend to be similar in the shape of the flower, the differences being mainly in colour. Hybrids with *P. equestris* in their ancestry have smaller flowers, but more of them. Hybrids of *P. schilleriana* have beautifully mottled leaves. The following is a very small selection of what is available.

WHITE
Allegria
Capitola 'Moonlight'
Doris
Gladys Read 'Snow Queen'
Happy Girl (white with a red lip)
Henriette Lecoufle 'Boule de Neige'

Phalaenopsis 'Golden Horizon Sunrise'

Mini Mark 'Maria Theresa', AAM/AOS (white with orange spots and an orange lip)
Opaline
Red Fan (white with a red lip)

PINK
Formosa Rose
Hilo Lip (pink with a white lip)
Hokuspocus
Lippeglut (dark pink lip)
Lipperose (dark pink lip)
Little Mary (dark pink lip)
Mistinguette (dotted with darker pink)
Party Dress
Patea 'Hawaii' (deep pink)
Romance
Sourire (pale to deep pink with mottled leaves)

YELLOW
Golden Amboin (spotted with brown)
Golden Buddha
Golden Emperor
Gorey 'Trinity'
Orchid World
Orglade's Lemon Dew
Sierra Gold 'Suzanne', FCC/AOS

RED
Cordova 'Ken's Ruby'
Ember 'East Red' (magenta)
Firelight 'Stone's River' (magenta)
Sophie Hausermann
Summer Morn 'Shari Mowlavi', AM/AOS

STRIPED
Hennessy (white or pink with red or pink stripes)
Modest Girl (white with pink stripes)
Nero Wolf (pink stripes with a darker pink, red lip)
Zuma Chorus (pink stripes on magenta)

Phragmipedium besseae

Phragmipedium

The South American slipper orchids are less widely cultivated than their Asiatic relatives, *Paphiopedilum*, but their popularity has increased in recent years. There are about 20 species in Central and South America that differ only in botanical detail from *Paphiopedilum*. Much of the current interest was stimulated by the discovery of the red-flowered *P. besseae* in Peru in 1981, followed in 1987 by the discovery of another form of the same species in Ecuador, and their subsequent use in hybridization.

They require similar conditions to *Paphiopedilum*, except that they seem to need more frequent watering. They should not be divided too often as they do better in big clumps.

P. besseae
has bright scarlet flowers about 6cm (2½in) in diameter. The variety *dalessandroi*, the form from Ecuador, has a more branched flower spike with more numerous, but slightly smaller, flowers

that are usually orange-red. Flowers appear in autumn.

P. longifolium

has a tall flower spike with several flowers opening over a long period. The flowers are yellow-green, the petals edged with purple, the lip with purple spots. It flowers off and on throughout the year.

P. pearcei

is a dwarf species from Ecuador and Peru, where it often grows on boulders in rivers. It has narrow, dark green leaves and green and purple flowers about 7.5cm (3in) in diameter, with ribbon-like, twisted petals.

P. schlimii

is a Colombian species with a branched or unbranched flower spike to 50cm (20in) high, with pink and white flowers.

Hybrids

Don Wimber very large orange flowers, produced freely.

Elizabeth March pink and white flowers .

Eric Young large, salmon to orange flowers.

Hanne Popow the first *P. besseae* hybrid to be registered, in 1992; the colour ranges from apricot to pale pink and deep pink.

Mem. Dick Clements a relatively compact plant with many deep red flowers. Other good reds include Living Fire, Ruby Slippers and Jason Fischer.

Sedenii an old hybrid made over 100 years ago with long-lasting pink and white flowers opening off and on for most of the year.

Polystachya bella

Polystachya

There are about 200 species of *Polystachya* found throughout the tropics but with most in Africa. They are small to medium plants, almost all epiphytic, with pseudobulbs varying from small and round to flat and coin-like or narrowly cylindrical. The long-lasting flowers are usually small with the lip held uppermost, in a range of colours; most are scented. Plants can be mounted on bark if the humidity is high enough, or potted in a fine bark mix that should be allowed to dry out between waterings.

Rhyncholaelia digbyana

P. bella

is a lovely species with golden yellow to orange flowers, known only from one area in Kenya but well established in cultivation. The pseudobulbs grow on an ascending stem so plants in pots should be given a branch or a moss pole to climb. It flowers off and on through the year.

P. campyloglossa

has very strongly and sweetly scented lime-green to yellow-green flowers with a white lip.

P. cultriformis

has conical, single-leafed pseudobulbs and branched spikes of numerous flowers in white, yellow or pale to deep pink.

P. fallax

is another very fragrant species with white and yellow flowers off and on throughout the year.

P. rosea

is a relatively tall species from Madagascar with an erect, branched flower spike up to 30cm (12in) high; the pink flowers are small but numerous.

Rhyncholaelia

A genus with two species of epiphytic orchid from Mexico and Central America, formerly included in *Brassavola*.

R. digbyana

(synonym *Brassavola digbyana*) has club-shaped pseudobulbs each with one stiff, grey-green leaf. The large, long-lasting flowers are scented, usually yellow-green; the lip is white or cream tinged with green, and the mid lobe is deeply fringed. Grow potted in a coarse mix in bright light.

Stanhopea

About 25 species of large epiphytic orchids from tropical America, with smallish pseudobulbs, each with one large, pleated leaf. The flowers are large, strangely shaped and strongly scented, but last for only two or three days. Because the flower spikes grow downwards, stanhopeas must be grown in baskets in a coarse bark mix. They like good light, a humid atmosphere and plenty of water while in growth.

S. oculata
has creamy yellow flowers with red blotches on each side of the lip base, in summer.
S. tigrinum
has bright orange flowers blotched with maroon-red.
S. wardii
has yellow flowers; the lip is orange with deep red-black eye spots on either side of the base.

Stanhopea oculata

Vanilla

A genus with about 100 species of scrambling and climbing orchids found throughout the tropics. The stems are green, stout and fleshy, with many roots. Some cling (like ivy) and some grow down until they reach the ground. Some species have large, fleshy leaves while others have only scale leaves and appear leafless. The flowers are large, usually with spreading sepals and petals and a trumpet-shaped lip, but are not usually produced until the plant has reached a considerable height. Plant in pots in a standard bark mix, with a long moss pole for the stem to climb – it should be tied to the pole to start with. When the top of the pole is reached, the stem can either be allowed to dangle (which sometimes stimulates flowering) or be trained horizontally along a pole parallel to the ridge of the greenhouse or conservatory. Even when not in flower, the plants look interesting.

Vanilla polylepis

V. planifolia

is the commercial vanilla, native to Central America and the West Indies but widely planted and often naturalized elsewhere, particularly in Madagascar. The capsules are still used to produce vanilla flavouring, far superior to synthetic vanilla essence. The flowers are yellow-green, about 10cm (4in) in diameter. There is a form with variegated leaves.

V. pompona

(synonym *V. grandiflora*) has leaves up to 25cm (10in) long and yellow-green flowers about 15cm (6in) in diameter with orange marks on the lip.

V. polylepis

is a tropical African species with very attractive flowers, white or greenish-white. The lip has a yellow blotch in the throat and is usually maroon-purple towards the apex.

The following orchids can be grown in the warmer parts of an intermediate greenhouse, but they will grow and flower better in a warm house.

Orchids for the warm greenhouse
minimum night-time temperature **18°C(65°F)**

9

Orchids for the warm greenhouse

Aerides

This genus includes about 20 species of monopodial epiphytes from Asia with showy spikes of scented flowers, usually white, pink or purplish. They are large plants that like warm, humid conditions so in spite of their striking display, they are not often grown in Europe. They have many long, aerial roots and do well in baskets.

A. multiflora
(synonym *A. affinis*) is a robust plant with leaves up to 30cm (12in) long, and large sprays of white or pink flowers in summer.

A. rosea
(synonym *A. fieldingii*) is similar to *A. multiflora* but with slightly larger purple flowers, tinged with white, in dense spikes up to 35cm (14in) long, which appear in summer.

Angraecum

Some species of *Angraecum* grow best in a warm greenhouse, although they will grow in the warmer parts of an intermediate house (see page 77).

A. eburneum
is a large, robust species with several pairs of leathery, strap-shaped leaves. The flower spikes are erect with up to 30 flowers with green sepals and petals and a white, shell-shaped lip which is held uppermost. There are four subspecies from different geographical areas that differ slightly in size and proportions of lip. Subspecies *superbum* is the largest and its variety *longicalcar* has probably the longest spur known in any orchid – up to 35cm (14in) long. *A. eburneum* likes good light; it is a striking plant, but large.

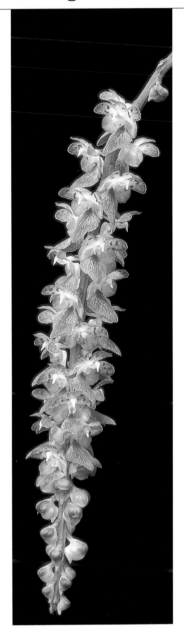

Aerides multiflora

Ascocentrum

This genus contains five species of epiphytic orchid resembling small vandas, occurring in Asia from India to the Philippines. The stems are erect, with two rows of leaves; the brightly coloured red, orange or pink flowers are in dense, erect spikes. Grow in pots or baskets in a medium to coarse bark mix or mounted on a slab. They like good light and high humidity and regular feeding and watering while in growth; keep drier in winter. They will grow in the warmer parts of an intermediate house, but are better in a warm house.

A. ampullaceum
is a compact species with bright cherry-pink flowers in spring. The variety *aurantiacum* has orange flowers.
A. curvifolium
is larger, with stems to 25cm (10in) long. The flowers are deep orange to red with a yellow lip and a purple column. An attractive species which has been widely used in hybridization.
A. garayi
has bright golden-orange flowers very freely borne.

Ascocentrum ampullaceum

Catasetum expansum

Catasetum

These are sympodial orchids, most epiphytic, from tropical Central and South America and the West Indies. Estimates of the number of species vary from 50 to 130. They are unusual among orchids in that the flowers are either male or female, usually carried on different plants but sometimes on the same plant. They often look very different; the male flowers are usually brightly coloured and the female flowers are usually yellow-green. All have fleshy pseudobulbs and large, pleated leaves, usually deciduous in winter. The flower spikes may be erect, arching or pendent. Grow in pots or baskets in a coarse bark compost, at intermediate or warm temperatures and in bright light. Give plenty of water and fertilizer while growing but in winter give only enough water to stop the pseudo-bulbs from shrivelling. Humidity should be high while plants are growing actively.

C. barbatum

usually has green male flowers with maroon spots and a hair-fringed lip. The female flowers are similar but smaller, without the fringe on the lip. Flowers appear in summer.

C. saccatum

is a variable species from Brazil, Peru and Guyana. The male flowers can be white, green, purple-brown, orange or purple; the female flowers are yellow-green. Flowers are borne in summer.

C. tenebrosum

has male flowers with maroon-brown sepals and a fleshy lip in yellow, lime green or purple. The female flowers are greenish-red. Flowers appear in summer.

Hybrids

Some fine *Catasetum* hybrids have been registered in recent years but few are widely available.

Orchidglade has yellow-green flowers very heavily mottled with maroon.

Dendrobium

Some species of *Dendrobium* need warm conditions throughout the year and although they, too, should be kept drier when not in active growth they should not remain dry for long periods. They can make good houseplants and seem to be particularly successful in a kitchen with an Aga or Rayburn cooker, which is always warm.

D. bigibbum

(synonym *D. phalaenopsis*) has stout, upright canes and arching spikes of about 20 white, lilac or pink flowers with a darker lip. It is found in New Guinea and Australia. Large-flowered forms were known as *D. phalaenopsis* but are now usually treated as *D. bigibbum* subsp. *phalaenopsis*. Many beautiful hybrids have been developed from this species and are important in East Asia for the cut-flower trade.

American Beauty magenta-purple flowers.

Bangkok Fancy lavender to purple flowers.

Dendrobium Thai Fancy

Candy Stripe pale pink flowers with deeper pink stripes.
Dale Takiguchi white flowers.
Doreen 'Kodama' white flowers.
Lady Fay magenta-purple flowers.
Lady Hamilton magenta-purple flowers.
Orglade's Orbit - magenta-purple flowers.

Doritis

There are two or three species of *Doritis* in East Asia; they are closely related to *Phalaenopsis*. These plants have short stems, stiff fleshy leaves, thick flattened roots and showy flowers. They grow well in pots or baskets with a medium bark compost and require plenty of water and fertilizer while in growth; even when resting, they should not dry out completely. *Doritis* species are grown less often than *Doritaenopsis*, their hybrids with *Phalaenopsis*.

D. pulcherrima
(synonym *D. esmeralda*) has a large flower spike, up to 60cm (24in) tall in summer; the numerous flowers are usually magenta but sometimes paler. The variety *coerulea* has blue-violet flowers.

Doritaenopsis
(Doritis x Phalaenopsis)

These are vigorous, free-flowering plants with characteristics halfway between the parents. The long-lasting flowers are white, pink or red, usually spotted or striped with a darker colour. The flowers appear on tall, often branched, spikes usually in summer.
Coral Gleam deep pink flowers.
Flame Mountain 'Zuma Boy' deep pink with red stripes.
George Moler white flowers striped with pink and a deep red lip.
Happy Valentine large pink flowers with a red or orange lip.
Krull's Dazzler 'Ponkans Cherries Jubilee', AM/AOS deep pink flowers with a darker lip.
Lady Jewel white flowers.
Orglade's Puff white flowers with gold marks on the lip.
Purple Gem 'Vivid' bright magenta flowers.
Red Coral deep pinkish-red flowers on branched stems.

Doritis pulcherrima

Euanthe

This genus includes one species of monopodial epiphyte from the Philippines, formerly included in *Vanda*.

E. sanderiana

(synonyms *Esmeralda sanderiana* and *Vanda sanderiana*) is a beautiful species with a tall, leafy stem with flower spikes arising from the leaf axils. The flat-faced flowers are 10cm (4in) in diameter and are pale to deep pink, with the lower half of the flower veined and streaked with purple-brown. Grow in a pot or basket in a coarse bark mix in good light, with plenty of water and feeding while in active growth but less in winter.

Psychopsis

These are the butterfly orchids. The genus includes about five species of epiphytes from Central and South America,

Psychopsis papilio

sometimes included in *Oncidium*, with clustered, single-leafed pseudobulbs and often mottled leaves. The erect or arching flower spikes bear showy flowers with a narrow, erect dorsal sepal and petals resembling antennae. The frilly lip is yellow and brown. Do not cut off old flower spikes even if they look as they have finished, because flowers may still be produced. Grow in a very open, coarse compost or mounted, in warm, shady, humid conditions.

P. papilio (synonym *Oncidium papilio* and *Oncidium picta*) has tall spikes, up to 1m (3ft) high or even more, each with many flowers. The yellow and brown striped flowers open one or two at a time over a long period.

Rhynchostylis

These are the foxtail orchids. The genus includes about six species of monopodial epiphytes from Asia. Stems are short, the roots long and numerous and the leaves thick and leathery. The flower spikes are usually pendent and cylindrical and bear many flowers. The flowers are white or pink, with purple markings. Because of their long roots and pendent spikes this species should be grown in baskets in a coarse, free-draining compost.

R. gigantea

has spikes up to 35cm (14in) long. The waxy flowers are about 3cm (1in) in diameter, usually white spotted with violet and purple, but pure white and rose-purple forms are known.

R. retusa

has flower spikes up to 45cm (18in) long, bearing small white flowers, spotted with pink and violet.

Tolumnia

Tolumnia includes about 20 species of small epiphyte from Central America and the West Indies, closely related to *Oncidium* and still usually referred to as the 'equitant' or 'variegata' oncidiums. They have no pseudobulbs and the leaves form a fan. The flowers are big for the size of plant with a large, usually four-lobed lip. It is best to mount the plants, as they rot easily if water lodges among the leaves, but with careful watering they can be grown in small pots in a very free-draining compost. They like good light, good air movement and high humidity.

T. pulchella
(synonym *Oncidium pulchellum*) has an arched spike bearing many white, pink or magenta flowers.

T. variegata
(synonym *Oncidium variegatum*) is slightly smaller with white or pink flowers marked with brown or crimson.

Vanda

This genus contains about 40 species of monopodial orchids from tropical Asia. The stems are usually long and leafy, with roots along their length and flower spikes arising in the leaf joints. The flat-faced flowers are showy. Plants are usually grown in baskets in a coarse, bark-based compost but in the Far East, where vandas are widely grown, they are often grown in baskets with no compost at all, the roots attaching themselves to the basket or hanging free. They like bright light and most prefer warm, or warm to intermediate temperatures.

V. coerulea
has a stem up to 1.5m (5ft) long. The flowers are about 10cm (4in) in diameter and pale to deep lilac-blue. This species comes from higher altitudes than most and can be grown in a cool greenhouse as it dislikes high winter temperatures. It flowers in autumn to winter.

V. coerulescens
is a much smaller plant than the last with the stem only about 10cm (4in) long. The flowers are 4cm (11/2in) in diameter, blue-violet with a darker lip.

V. tricolor
(synonym *V. suavis*) has a stem up to 1m (3ft) tall. The flowers are scented, 8cm (3in) in diameter and usually white or pale yellow spotted with red-brown. The lip is magenta and white. Flowers appear in autumn and winter.

Hybrids
Many beautiful hybrids are available but because of their size and their need for high temperatures, they are much more widely grown in the Far East than in Europe or most of America. There are many hybrids with *Ascocentrum* – see *Ascocenda* (page 79).

Vanda Miss Joachim a tall plant with cylindrical leaves and lavender flowers with a large, dark rose pink lip.

Vanda Rothschildiana a compact but vigorous plant with large, deep lavender blue flowers with darker chequering, appearing in winter.

Vanda Rothschildiana

Orchids that do well in an alpine house include those that can withstand low but not freezing temperatures and also those that can survive sub-zero temperatures but dislike winter wet. All these plants also do well in an unheated conservatory.

Orchids for the alpine house

minimum night-time temperature **0°C(32°F)**

10

Bletilla

This genus includes about 10 species of terrestrial orchids from Japan and China, which are almost hardy in temperate climates. They have corm-like pseudobulbs and deciduous, pleated leaves and will grow in any well-drained, peat-based or loam-based compost if it is alkaline

B. striata

(synonym *B. hyacinthina*) is by far the most common species in cultivation, sometimes sold in garden centres. The flowers are rose-purple and grow on an erect spike that appears from between the leaves in early summer. There is a white form with a yellow throat, but this is much less easy to obtain.

Calanthe

The deciduous calanthes have already been described (see page 82). While evergreen species can be either tropical or temperate, it is the temperate ones that are more often grown. They are almost hardy and do well in alpine house conditions. They grow in any free-draining terrestrial compost and need plenty of water while in growth but should be kept drier, but not completely dry, in winter. Several are native to Japan, where they are popular plants.

C. discolor

is a spring-flowering Japanese species with a flower spike 40–50cm (16–20in) tall. The flowers are either white, pink or maroon with a pink lip.

C. reflexa

is a small, spring-flowering Japanese species with the flower spikes reaching only 15cm (6in) high. The flowers are white, pink or magenta with a darker lip and a yellow base.

Bletilla striata

C. striata

(synonym *C. sieboldii*) is another Japanese species with the flower spikes growing up to 45cm (18in) tall, bearing large, yellow flowers in early summer.

Cymbidium

One or two species of *Cymbidium* are hardy enough to be grown out of doors in a sheltered spot, but it is safer to grow them in an alpine house or as a house plant. Use the same composts and general cultivation methods as for the other cymbidiums described in Chapter 7 (see page 55).

C. goeringii,

native to China and Japan, is believed to have been cultivated in China for over 2,000 years and in Japan for many hundreds of years. Many varieties are available there. It has dark green, grassy leaves and flowers borne singly on a stalk 10–15cm (4–6in) long. The flowers open in winter or spring and are about 5cm (2in) in diameter and sometimes scented. They are green, yellow-green, brown or brownish-orange with a white lip marked with red or purple.

Ophrys

This genus contains 30–50 species of tuberous terrestrial orchid occurring in Europe, North Africa and the Middle East, with most from the Mediterranean region. Four species are British natives. They are plants that always attract attention as the flowers mimic various female insects so effectively that the males try to mate with them and, in so doing, carry pollen from one flower to another. A few species are now available from specialist nurseries; they can be grown in the open garden but are more often grown in pots in an alpine house. Drainage must be good and most species require a hot, dry summer to do well. After flowering in spring and summer, plants die back until rosettes of leaves appear in late winter. In the wild, most species grow on chalk and limestone, so dolomitic limestone or limestone chips should be added to the compost. A recommended *Ophrys* compost is three parts of sterile loam to three parts of coarse gritty sand, two parts of sieved beech or oak leafmould and one part of fine pine bark, plus some limestone chips and a little hoof and horn fertilizer.

O. apifera

the bee orchid, is widespread in Europe. It has pink sepals and petals and a furry brown and green lip.

O. fusca

is a Mediterranean species that is supposed to be one of the easier species in cultivation. It grows 10–40cm (4–16in) tall, with green to yellow sepals, yellow to brown petals and a dark brown lip.

O. insectifera

the fly orchid is a British native, a slender plant with green sepals, black antenna-like petals and a furry dark brown lip with a blue base.

Pleione

This genus includes about 20 mainly terrestrial species found from India east to Taiwan and Thailand. They used to be known as windowsill orchids, but as so

Pleione bulbocodioides

many other kinds of orchids are now grown indoors, that name is less appropriate than it was. They produce clumps of pseudobulbs, each with one or two leaves. The flowers are showy and large for the size of the plant, in white, pink, mauve or yellow, usually with darker markings on the lip.

Most species are hardy down to 0°C (32°F) and so in theory they could be grown out of doors in milder areas. They do not, however, like winter wet and are much better indoors or in an alpine house over winter, although they can be put outside in a shady, sheltered place in summer. Plant them in shallow pots, preferably terracotta. Numerous different composts are used, but as for all terrestrial orchids, the most important factor is that it is free-draining. One suitable mix consists of six parts of fine orchid bark to one part of coarse perlite or perlag, one part of chopped sphagnum moss and one part of chopped bracken fronds or chopped freshly fallen oak or beech leaves.

The pseudobulbs should be cleaned up and repotted in January or February. Trim the old roots down to about 1cm (1/2in) long and cut away any old, loose sheaths. Plant the pseudobulbs close together and just deep enough to anchor them in the compost. Keep at a temperature of 0–10°C (32–50°F) until you see the flower buds emerging, then bring indoors and start to water carefully. When the flowers are over, the leaves grow rapidly so water and a balanced fertilizer can be given freely.

In July, change to a fertilizer that is higher in phosphate and potassium to encourage flowering the following year. When the leaves turn yellow and fall, the plants should be kept dry until you repot the following January.

Two species, *P. praecox* and *P. maculata*, and a few hybrids derived from them, flower in autumn but are treated in the same way as spring-flowering plants. All the species and hybrids of *Pleione* are rather similar in general appearance, with spreading sepals and petals and a fringed, trumpet-shaped lip. The flower spike is rarely taller than 20cm (8in) and bears one or two flowers.

P. bulbocodioides
has lilac-pink to magenta flowers with purple-brown marks on the lip. There is a pretty white form.

P. x confusa
is a natural hybrid of *P. forrestii*, with larger and often paler flowers.

P. formosana
has pale or mid lilac-pink flowers, the lip paler with yellow marks. This is the most common species in cultivation and there are numerous cultivars, including 'Blush of Dawn' and 'Oriental Splendour'. 'Clare' and 'Snow White' have white flowers.

P. forrestii
has yellow flowers, the lip spotted with brown or red.

P. speciosa
has purplish pseudobulbs and bright magenta flowers; the lip has pale orange markings and yellow crests.

Hybrids
More and more hybrids are becoming available; they are often more vigorous and free-flowering than the species from which they are derived.

Alishan lilac flowers, lip white with red marks. 'Goldfinch', 'Merlin' and 'Sparrowhawk' are good cultivars.

Eiger white flowers.

El Pico mauve to deep rose-purple flowers.

Shantung usually yellow or creamy white flowers flushed with pink. 'Fieldfare' has large, pale yellow flowers; 'Muriel Harberd' has large, apricot flowers.

Stromboli deep rose-purple flowers with an orange-blotched lip. 'Fireball' has particularly intense colouring.

Tolima mauve to deep pink flowers.

Tongariro purple flowers, marked with red and yellow; 'Jackdaw' has the deepest colour.

Versailles the first *Pleione* hybrid. The flowers are pale to deep pink; 'Bucklebury' flowers very freely.

Pterostylis

Pterostylis includes about 80 species of terrestrial orchids known as greenhoods; almost all are found in Australia and New Zealand. The flowers are green, often tinged with purple, and the uppermost sepal is arched and forms a hood with the petals. Some species are almost hardy in temperate climates but do not tolerate winter wet, so they are best grown in an alpine house or cool greenhouse. They dislike chalk and are usually grown in a compost mixture such as two parts of gritty sand to one part of sterile loam, one part of fine orchid bark and a sprinkling of bonemeal.

Plants are dormant in summer, the leaves appear in autumn and plants continue to grow throughout the winter. Some species form colonies in the wild and increase rapidly in cultivation. After flowering, keep the compost dry and resume watering with care when new growths start to appear.

P. cucullata is a colony-forming species with brown or brown and green flowers in early spring.

P. curta is a species that increases quickly. It grows to 30cm (12in) tall and has whitish flowers veined with green and tinged with brown, which open in late summer.

Pleione Shantung 'Ridgeway'

Quite a number of orchids are hardy
enough to be grown in temperate
gardens. Most like a well-drained
soil that does not dry out completely.
Orchids can be established in a
lawn and in fact they sometimes
establish themselves.

Orchids for the garden
minimum night-time temperature **10°C(50°F)**

11

Orchids for the garden

Orchids look great in the garden, and many are relatively easy to cultivate. A wildflower meadow can be created with lesser butterfly orchids (*Platanthera bifolia*), heath spotted orchids (*Dactylorhiza maculata* subsp. *ericetorum*) and northern marsh orchids (*Dactylorhiza purpurella*), for example. On chalky soil, autumn lady's tresses (*Spiranthes spiralis*) will sometimes appear spontaneously in lawns and tennis courts. Where orchids are growing in grass, management of the grass is important as the orchids are easily choked out. The grass should be cut (or grazed) in spring before the flowers start to develop, and then left alone until the flowers have faded and the seed has been shed. Then cutting or grazing can be resumed until the following spring.

Orchids can be erratic in their appearance; they may grow in profusion one year, then for no apparant reason, in far fewer numbers the next year. Terrestrial orchids seem able to persist underground for many years. When a piece of grassland that has been over-grazed or, conversely, allowed to grow rank is properly managed once again, orchids often reappear within a couple of years.

While some of the larger species of *Dactylorhiza*, such as *D. foliosa*, the Madeira orchid, seem to enjoy a rich, border soil, most wild orchids are happier in soil of low fertility. In the past, the main obstacle to growing hardy orchids in the garden was lack of availability but now several nurseries offer seed-grown plants of an increasing range of species.

These establish much more readily than plants lifted from the wild, a practice that is, in any case, against the law in most countries. In cold areas, several of the orchids mentioned below, such as species of *Orchis*, are more satisfactory grown in an alpine house.

Cypripedium

Some species of lady's slippers can be grown in gardens. As with other species of hardy terrestrial orchids, interest is increasing and seed-grown plants are becoming more widely available.

C. acaule,
the moccasin flower, is a summer-flowering North American species with brownish sepals and petals and a deep pink lip. It can be temperamental in cultivation.

C. calceolus,
the lady's slipper orchid, is hovering on the edge of extinction in Britain but is still relatively common in other countries. It has maroon-brown (occasionally green) sepals and petals and a bright yellow lip. It does not like acid soil.

Cypripedium parviflorum var. *pubescens*

C. parviflorum

(also known as *C. calceolus* var. *parviflorum*) is the North American form of *C. calceolus* and has at times been treated as a variety of that species. The summer flowers are smaller than those of *C. calceolus* but the colouring is similar: sepals and petals are purple to maroon, the lip yellow with red spots inside. Two varieties are recognized: var. *parviflorum* and var. *pubescens*. Both grow well in gardens in a good but well-drained soil and will form good clumps when established. They are probably the easiest species of *Cypripedium* to cultivate and, unlike *C. calceolus*, will grow in acid soils.

C. reginae,

the queen lady's slipper orchid, is a very handsome North American species with white or pale pink flowers with a deeper pink lip. In the wild, it grows in bogs but in cultivation it prefers a well-drained soil. The flowers appear in summer.

Dactylorhiza

These are the easiest of the hardy orchids to grow in most gardens. There are about 40 species, many rather similar, which are widespread in Europe, extending into Asia, with one or two in North America. They are closely related to *Orchis* but differ in having tubers with finger-like projections. Most grow well in a good, well-drained garden soil, preferably in light shade, and flower in summer. More species are now becoming available from seed-grown plants and any that can be obtained are worth growing. Several hybrids are starting to appear on the market and they seem to be even more vigorous than the species.

D. elata

is a handsome species native to South West Europe and North Africa, but it seems to be hardy in almost all temperate gardens. Plants have plain green leaves and tall, dense heads of rich purple flowers in summer. They increase well to form good clumps.

D. foliosa,

the Madeira orchid, grows wild only on the island of Madeira. It is a beautiful species, very similar to *D. elata*, differing mainly in lip shape, and grows and increases well in similar situations.

D. fuchsii,

the common spotted orchid, is an attractive species that is widespread in Britain. It has spotted leaves and pale to deep lilac-pink flowers with darker spots, in late spring or early summer. It grows taller and more luxuriantly in gardens than in the wild. Although it often grows on chalk, it also grows well on neutral to slightly acid soils.

D. maculata

subsp. *ericetorum*, the heath spotted orchid, occurs on more acid soils. It is a smaller plant than *D. fuchsii* with a shorter flower spike, but is also a pretty little plant.

Dactylorhiza fuchsii

Epipactis gigantea

Epipactis

This genus includes over 20 species of terrestrial orchids, mostly temperate but a few tropical, with creeping stems and fleshy roots. The following can be grown in the open garden.

E. gigantea

is a North American species with a rather misleading name as it is not very big. The stems are leafy, 30–60cm (12–24in) tall, with yellow-brown flowers striped with pink or purple which appear in late spring and summer. It increases well in light shade, in a soil which is well drained but does not dry out completely.

E. palustris,

the marsh helleborine, is a British native similar to the last species. The sepals are purplish-brown, the petals white tinged with pink at the base, and the lip white marked with yellow. It likes a fairly damp situation, preferably not in acid soil.

Orchis

Orchis contains about 30 species of terrestrial orchid with ovoid tubers, occurring in Europe and temperate Asia, as far east as China. There are seven British native species, although most are rare. A few can be grown in an open garden, either in a rock garden or naturalized in grass. However, most growers have them in pots in an alpine house, using a similar compost to that given for *Ophrys* (see page 114).

O. mascula,

the early purple orchid, is the most common of the British species, growing 15–60cm (6–24in) tall with leaves heavily spotted with purple. The light purple flowers have darker spots and appear in dense spikes in spring.

O. laxiflora,

the lax-flowered orchid, is fairly widespread in Europe. It is a tall plant with a loose spike of rose-pink or lilac flowers in spring and early summer.

O. morio,

the green-veined orchid, used to be common in Britain but is now much rarer. It varies from 5–50cm (2–20in) tall and usually has whitish or purplish sepals and petals veined with purple and green, and a purple lip. It flowers in spring and early summer. This is one of those species that sometimes appears in lawns and anyone who is lucky enough to have a colony should be careful not to mow the grass until seed has been shed, usually at about the end of July or early in August.

Axil – the angle between a leaf and a stem

Bifoliate – with two leaves

Bract – a small leaf at the base of a flower stem or flower spike

Callus – a protruberance or growth, usually on the lip of an orchid

Clone – the asexually produced offspring of a single parent; they will be genetically identical

Column – in an orchid, the organ formed by the fusion of stamens, style and stigma

Cultivar – a particular form of a species or hybrid

Epiphyte – a plant which grows on another plant, but without obtaining nourishment from it

Genus (plural genera) – a natural group of closely related species

Grex – a group name for all plants derived from a cross between the same two species or hybrids

Intergeneric – between or among two or more genera

Intrageneric – within one genus

Keiki – a small plant arising from the stem, pseudobulb or inflorescence of a mature plant

Lip (labellum) – the unpaired petal of an orchid

Lithophyte – a plant which grows on a rock

Meristem – undifferentiated tissue, usually from a growing point, which is capable of developing into specialized tissue, used in mass propagation of orchids

Ovary – the part of a flower which contains the ovules and eventually becomes the fruit, containing seed

Pollinarium – the male reproductive part of an orchid flower, consisting of the pollinia from an anther with the associated parts, the viscidium and stipes

Pollinium (plural pollinia) – pollen grains cohering into a mass

Protocorm – A swollen, tuber-like structure that is the first stage of growth after an orchid seed germinates

Pseudobulb – a swollen, bulb–like structure at the base of a stem

Rhizome – a stem on or below the ground with roots growing down from it and flowering shoots up

Rupicolous – rock-dwelling

Species – a group of similar individuals, the basic unit of classification

Spur – a slender, usually hollow, extension of a flower, usually from the lip but in *Disa*, formed from the dorsal sepal

Stigma – the part of the column which receives pollen

Stipe or stipes (plural stipites) – a stalk joining the pollinium to the viscidium

Stolon – a running stem which forms roots

Synonym – botanically, another name for the same species which is now considered invalid

Terrestrial – growing in the ground

Unifoliate – with one leaf

Velamen – an absorbent layer of cells covering the roots of many orchids

Cover pictures: **Octopus Publishing Group Ltd.**/Mark Winwood

A-Z Botanical Collection 100, 98 Top, /Jiri Loun 99, 106 Bottom, /Terry Mead 17 Top, /Dan Sams 79, /Silvia Sroka 115, /Malkolm Warrington 118, 121, /Andy Williams 56 Top Left; **Adrian Bloom Horticultural Library**/Javier Delgado 16, 17 Bottom, 21, Professor Stefan Buczacki 35 left, 39; **Corbis UK Ltd**/Hal Horwitz 70 Top, 70 Bottom, 106 Top, /Kevin Schafer 67; **Eric Crichton** 59, 72 Top, 85; **DAC Photographics** 3, 36 left, 65, 78 right, 82, 109, 117; **Deni Bown** 69; **Garden Picture Library**/Mark Bolton 98 Bottom; **Garden & Wildlife Matters** 32, 36 right, 37 Bottom Right; **John Glover** 96 Top; **Octopus Publishing Group Ltd.** /John Sims 34, /Mark Winwood 1, 2, 4, 5, 10, 12 Bottom Right, 23, 24, 25, 26, 40, 41 Top, 41 Bottom, 42 Top, 42 Bottom, 43, 45, 48, 50, 54, 57, 58, 74, 84 Top, 92 Top, 92 Bottom, 94 Top, 97 Top, 104, 107, 112; **Harpur Garden Library**/Jerry Harpur 9, 56 Bottom Right, 72 Bottom, 80, 111, /Marcus Harpur 68 Top; **E.A.S. la Croix** 12 Top Left, 12 Top Right, 13 Top, 13 Bottom Right, 14, 62, 63, 76 Bottom, 77 Top, 83, 86 left, 86 right, 87, 89 Top, 89 Bottom, 93, 94 Bottom, 96 Bottom, 103, 120, 61, 91, 113; **Andrew Lawson** 119; **S & O Mathews** 55, 95 Top; **N.H.P.A.**/N.A.Callow 37 Top Right, /Kevin Schafer 101; **Oxford Scientific Films**/Raymond Blythe 64, /Deni Bown 77 Bottom, 84 Bottom, 102, /Peter Gould 73, /Geoff Kidd 60, 78 left, 81, 105, /R.L.Manuel 11, 20, 66, 71 Top, 76 Top, /Edward Parker 13 Bottom Left, /Kjell B Sandved 108; **Photos Horticultural** 27, 71 Bottom, 75, 68 Bottom, 90 Top, 90 Bottom; **Royal Horticultural Society** 53; **Science Photo Library**/Dr Jeremy Burgess 35 right, 37 left; **Harry Smith Collection** 88, 95 Bottom, 97 Bottom, 38.

AUTHOR'S ACKNOWLEDGEMENTS

I should like to thank my husband Eric, Joyce Stewart and Geoff Hands for help and advice in various ways.